A PRIMER
ON SUSTAINABLE
BUILDING

ROCKY MOUNTAIN INSTITUTE
GREEN DEVELOPMENT SERVICES
DIANNA LOPEZ BARNETT
WITH WILLIAM D. BROWNING

Rocky Mountain Institute is a nonprofit research and educational foundation with a vision across boundaries. Seeking ideas that transcend ideology, and harnessing the problem-solving power of free-market economics, our goal is to foster the efficient and sustainable use of resources as a path to global security.

Rocky Mountain Institute's work on environmentally responsive development is coordinated by Green Development Services. This program promotes sustainable development to the building industry through three components: research into the cost, approvals, construction, and market implications of environmentally responsive development; direct consulting services to architects, planners, developers, and corporations on the implications and methods of environmentally responsive development; and information services to such professional organizations as the American Institute of Architects and the U.S. Green Building Council.

RMI does not endorse any products or businesses, including any listed in this book. While we have attempted to provide comprehensive and detailed information related to the issues of energy efficiency and sustainable design, the information provided in this book cannot and does not replace the services of competent registered architects, engineers and other design professionals. Please feel free to help us correct any errors, inaccuracies, or omissions for future editions.

Book Design: Dan Sadowsky/Flying Color
Desktop Publisher: Kate Mink
Illustrators: Dianna Lopez Barnett and Jenifer Seal

ROCKY MOUNTAIN INSTITUTE
A PRIMER ON SUSTAINABLE BUILDING

TABLE OF CONTENTS

ACKNOWLEDGMENTS

This book could not have been prepared without the generous assistance of the many architects, builders, and other experts who so unselfishly shared their expertise. Our thanks to all, particularly those who reviewed an earlier draft: Clark Atkinson of Shaw Construction, Grand Junction, CO; Greg Franta, FAIA, of ENSAR Group, Boulder, CO; Helen Kessler, AIA, of Sieben Energy Associates, Chicago, IL; Gail Lindsey, AIA, of Design Harmony, Raleigh, NC; Mona Newton of Boulder Energy Conservation Center, Boulder, CO; Ed Troyer, AIA, Glenwood Springs, CO; Peter Vogel of AR18 Designs, Los Angeles, CA; and Alex Wilson of *Environmental Building News*, Brattleboro, VT. Any errors or omissions, however, are ours.

Many Rocky Mountain Institute staff members also helped make this book possible. Special thanks to Owen Bailey for research, Kathleen Mink for layout development and research, Jenifer Seal for illustrations, John Barnett, Guy Harrington, L. Hunter Lovins, and Randy Udall for editing assistance, and Jeanette Darnauer for helping to edit, publish, and promote this work. Special thanks to Dan Sadowsky and the staff of Flying Color for their indispensable design help. Much of the information in this Primer is based on the groundbreaking work in energy efficiency conducted over the past twenty years by Amory B. Lovins, the Institute's Director of Research. This book was made possible by funding from the Educational Foundation of America.

PROLOGUE

This Primer, compiled by recognized leaders in the ever-growing field of sustainable design, serves as a comprehensive guide to sustainable building principles. It is a must for those who wish to positively affect the lives of future generations by the way that they choose to build and develop throughout this land. The principles and ideas presented within this document are both easily understood and of immense value to professionals in the building industry as well as interested individuals. Combined with the comprehensive appendices containing lists of source materials and relevant organizations, this Primer is a cornerstone for any sustainable building project.

—SUSAN MAXMAN, FAIA
1993 PRESIDENT OF THE AMERICAN INSTITUTE OF ARCHITECTS

The logic of sustainable development and its economic benefits to developers, builders, consumers, and government have been hidden behind a veil of doing the same old thing and the view that sustainable building is not cost effective. This book reminds us that many of the principles of sustainable development are old principles put aside over the last fifty years. It also brings to light the many practicable examples of how sustainable principles create a healthier environment of business. Most importantly, it teaches us a way of thinking and analysis that enables us to find our own way to becoming sustainable designers, developers, or builders.

—JOHN L. KNOTT, JR.
1976-78 NATIONAL CHAIRMAN OF THE
NATIONAL ASSOCIATION OF HOME BUILDERS
REMODELING AND REHABILITATION DIVISION

A PHOENIX RISING
A TRUE PARABLE OF SUSTAINABLE DESIGN

We entered a design competition to build a high-rise in Warsaw, Poland. When the client chose our design as the winner after seeing the model, we said, "We're not finished yet. We have to tell you all about the building. The concrete base includes tiny bits of rubble from World War II. It looks like limestone, but the rubble's there for visceral reasons." And he said, "I understand, a phoenix rising." And we said, "The skin is recycled aluminum," and he said, "That's fine." And we said, "The floor heights are thirteen feet clear so that we can convert the building into housing in the future, when its utility as an office building is no longer." And he said, "That's OK." And we told him that we would have operable windows and that no one would be further than twenty-five feet from one, and he said that was OK, too. And finally, we said, "By the way, you have to plant ten square miles of forest to offset the building's effect on climate change." We had calculated the energy costs to build the structure and the energy cost to run it, and it worked out that 6,400 acres of trees would offset the effects on climate change from the energy requirements. And he said he would get back to us. He called back two days later and said, "You still win. I checked out what it would cost to plant ten square miles of trees in Poland and it turns out it's equivalent to a small part of the advertising budget."

—WILLIAM McDONOUGH, AIA
A LEADING PRACTITIONER OF GREEN DESIGN,
DESCRIBING ONE OF HIS PROJECTS.[1]

INTRODUCTION

"I have endeavored to put together, and teach easily with words and figures, all these things that seemed to me most necessary, and most important for building well…that they may in themselves contain beauty, and be of credit and conveniency to the owners."
—ANDREA PALLADIO, ARCHITECT, ~ 1570

Thirty years ago, architectural critic and social commentator Lewis Mumford noted that "…the modern architect has produced the most flagrantly uneconomic and uncomfortable buildings…which can be inhabited only with the aid of the most expensive devices of heating and refrigeration. The irrationality of this system of construction is visible today in every city from New York to San Francisco: glass-sheathed buildings without any contact with fresh air, sunlight, or view."[2]

More recently, England's Prince Charles, a well-known architectural critic, stated, "We have suffered too long from a kind of non-descript, mediocre, synthetic, international style of architecture which is found everywhere from Riyadh to Rangoon. Our own heritage of regional styles and individual characteristics has been eaten away by this creeping cancer."[3]

The stylistic corruption decried by Prince Charles is symptomatic of a much deeper problem: Many of today's buildings, construction practices, and land use patterns are not sustainable. They don't work very well now, and they won't work at all in the long run.

Although today's buildings are more resource-efficient than those of thirty years ago, the average house, office, school, apartment building, or hotel still places undue demands on the earth, wasting tremendous amounts of energy and water. Sited and designed with little regard for local climate, new buildings are far more expensive to heat or cool than necessary. Meanwhile, leapfrogging, sprawling development erodes existing communities, converts prime farm lands to housing, requires expensive new highways for commuters, and exacts a heavy toll on the environment.

Today's buildings not only are designed without the planet in mind; they also neglect their occupants. The news is sprinkled with stories about "sick" office buildings whose air quality makes workers ill. Office workers often toil in bleak spaces with windows that won't open and lighting that is poor. Homeowners pick up the tab for energy-inefficient construction and drafty houses.

Although unsustainable buildings' harm may appear to be localized, it actually ripples outwards, sometimes for thousands of miles. Philippine forests are clear-cut for plywood used to build offices in Japan, where sheets used to form concrete are typically thrown away after one use. Homes in Southern California are framed with old-growth lumber from Washington and powered by burning coal strip-mined from Navajo sacred lands in Arizona. Ultimately, the costs of poor design are borne not solely by a building's owner and those who work and live there, but by everyone.

As growing numbers of homeowners, architects, builders, and developers realize the need for change, an exciting new field is emerging. It is called "sustainable design" or "green development." Although this new architecture is difficult to describe in a sentence or two, its overall goal is to produce buildings that take less from the earth and give more to people.

Note that sustainable design is not a new building *style*. Instead, it represents a revolution in how we think about, design, construct, and operate buildings. The primary goal of sustainable design is to lessen the harm poorly designed buildings cause by using the best of ancient building approaches in logical combination with the best of new technological advances. Its ultimate goal is to make possible offices, homes, even entire subdivisions, that are net *producers* of energy, food, clean water and air, beauty, and healthy human and biological communities.

Although the building industry is by nature a conservative one, the principles of sustainable design are simple and the advantages of green buildings compelling. This healing type of architecture seems destined to be the wave of the future. Already, in Europe, Japan, and the United States, the number of green building projects is growing exponentially. The American Institute of Architects' and the International Union of Architects' recent *Declaration of Interdependence for a Sustainable Future* endorses the concept. Within two decades or less, sustainable design will be standard practice. But why wait that long? If you're a builder, architect, developer, or owner, this book will give you that future now. The glossary in the back of this Primer will help to clarify some of the new terms and concepts associated with sustainable building and design. Also included in Appendix B is a comprehensive list of source information and organizations related to sustainable building and design.

> *"Never doubt that a small group of thoughtful committed citizens can change the world. Indeed it's the only thing that ever has."*
> —MARGARET MEAD, ANTHROPOLOGIST, ~ 1958

The concepts presented here are most relevant for the design of houses and other buildings that do not exceed 50,000 square feet in size; an average new home is about 2,100. Such buildings are said to be "climate-dominated"—that is, the amount of energy it takes to heat or cool them is controlled by heat loss or gain through the foundation, walls, and roof.

This information is broadly applicable to all sites and all climates. Although it almost goes without saying, every building should be designed with site and climate in mind: a builder in frigid Alaska will do things differently than one in semi-tropical Florida. But the general principles of green development will apply to most sites and climates.

The staff of Green Development Services at Rocky Mountain Institute has written this Primer for architects and their clients, home builders, developers, contractors, landscape architects, owner-builders, and others in the construction industry. If you plan to erect a new building, retrofit an existing one, even design an entire subdivision or new town, and you are also concerned about resale value, utility bills, human health, the environment, or simply saving money, this book is for you.

THE NEED FOR SUSTAINABLE DESIGN

*"What is the use of a house if you haven't got
a tolerable planet to put it on?"*
—HENRY DAVID THOREAU, PHILOSOPHER, ~ 1854

The Long Haul

*The phrase "sustainable" is fast
becoming a buzzword, but what does it
really mean? Here's one simple
definition from the writer Robert
Gilman: "Sustainability refers to a very
old and very simple concept—the
ability to keep going over the long
haul. Think of it as extending the
Golden Rule through time, so that you
do unto future generations as you
would have them do unto you."*

In 1845, when Thoreau was building his famous cabin at Walden Pond, the US. population was a tenth its current size, forests were largely intact, and human structures of all kinds were much smaller and less energy-intensive. In that simpler time, when the world's resources seemed infinite, the environmental impact of buildings could largely be ignored. We no longer have that luxury.

Modern houses use far more energy and water than Thoreau could ever have imagined. In truth, the biggest "guzzlers" in America are not cars, but *homes*. In 1990, for example, American households consumed $110 billion worth of energy. As houses consume lumber, energy, and other resources, they excrete wastes. The average household now produces each year about 3,500 pounds of garbage, 450,000 gallons of wastewater, and 25,000 pounds of CO_2 along with smaller amounts of SO_2, NO_x, and heavy metals.

By now, every builder and architect is familiar with the endless litany of environmental problems the world faces: population growth, air pollution, global warming, landfill shortages, deforestation... the list goes on. In recent years, reflections of these issues have begun to show up at the lumberyard in the form of new products and higher prices. Aerosol foams for plugging leaks are marketed as "ozone-friendly," and a few are even "ozone-safe." Lumber prices leap upwards in response to federal decisions to protect forests or stop below-cost timber sales. (Certainly, it would be hard today to build a cabin for the $28.12 Thoreau spent.)

As architectural issues and environmental issues become intertwined and as more consumers demand buildings that are cheaper to heat and cool, nicer to live in, and more earth-friendly, the time for green buildings has come.

As an architect, builder, or developer, you can use the principles of sustainable design to capitalize on this trend, to distinguish your projects in the marketplace, to save money, and to waste fewer resources, all the while doing your share to preserve the environment.

Applying that idea to construction yields a checklist of criteria that a sustainable building should meet. Ideally, such a building would:

- make appropriate use of land.
- use water, energy, lumber, and other resources efficiently.
- enhance human health.
- strengthen local economies and communities.
- conserve plants, animals, endangered species, and natural habitats.
- protect agricultural, cultural, and archaeological resources.
- be nice to live in.
- be economical to build and operate.

I. WHY GO GREEN?

"It's not easy being green."
—KERMIT THE FROG, ~1972

The reasons are numerous. Although green buildings cost about the same as conventional ones, their improved aesthetics, comfort, and performance translate into higher initial sales prices and rents, and then into lower operating costs. Green buildings are much cheaper to heat, cool, and light. Because they consume so much less energy, they produce correspondingly less pollution. Lower utility bills make them more affordable. Last but not least, they are healthier spaces in which to work or live—important now that typical Americans spend 80% of their time indoors.

MARKET PERFORMANCE AND ECONOMICS

The economic argument for sustainable buildings is compelling. In a housing market dominated by tract homes, consumers find distinctive green buildings eminently desirable. For example, home prices in the nation's oldest green neighborhood—Village Homes in Davis, California—now command $11 more per square foot than homes nearby.[4] Homes in a green development in Sacramento sell for $15,000 more than homes in adjoining subdivisions built by the same developer and builders.[5] This is not merely a California phenomenon: the Green Builder Program in Austin, Texas, has demonstrated that consumers there are willing to pay a premium for green homes.

The advantages of going green are not limited to home builders and buyers. Many business owners have discovered that shoppers patronize stores built with them and the earth in mind. Consider, for example, Wal-Mart's experimental "Eco-Mart" in Lawrence, Kansas.[6] In its first few months, the store's daylit half has shown a substantially higher sales rate than the conventionally lit side. A green building can even help a company increase its market share. The once-stodgy image of NMB, a Netherlands bank, was transformed after it constructed a widely acclaimed headquarters, complete with indoor waterfalls. This one-half-million-square-foot building uses one-tenth the energy per square foot of the bank's former building. Since moving in, NMB has become the second-largest bank in the country—in large part due to the change in public perception created by the building's architecture.

Green buildings also offer advantages to landlords. Reduced water and energy costs allow for a larger profit margin or more competitive leasing arrangements. Typical savings in annual operating costs of $1 per square foot can be used for rent concessions or for improvements to attract and retain tenants. Since leasing brokers often compete over 5 or 10 cents per square foot, efficiency is a remarkable leveraging tool.[7]

Because of such benefits, dozens of businesses have discovered the advantages of green buildings, including The Body Shop, Compaq Computer, the National Audubon Society, Natural Resources Defense Council, Sony, West Bend Mutual Insurance, and Verifone.

REDUCED RESOURCE CONSUMPTION

A green building or development will be much more resource-efficient than a conventional building or development of similar size. A 50% reduction in energy use is relatively easy to achieve, and 80 to 90% reductions are possible with good design.[8]

Making buildings efficient saves money and the environment. For example, saving one unit of electricity inside a building saves having to burn three or four units of fuel, often coal, at the power plant. Reducing the average house's energy use by 80% will reduce its CO_2 emissions by almost 90,000 pounds over its 30-year lifetime. Reducing water use by 30% would avoid the creation of over 4 million gallons of wastewater during the same period.[9]

Green developments also make wise use of other natural resources. Poorly designed or sited buildings scar the landscape, take valuable agricultural lands out of production, and diminish wildlife habitat. Green projects, on the other hand, can restore and enhance natural habitats, preserving valuable landscapes while adding to the marketable amenities of the project. The elegant design of new buildings, in concert with the imaginative reuse of old ones, can significantly

A Tale of Two Oases

A human presence can be beneficial to wildlife. Consider two desert springs 30 miles apart near Tucson. Until 1957, both oases were home to Papago Indians who farmed and raised fruit trees there. In that year, the National Park Service evicted the Papago from one oasis to create a "bird sanctuary." When the Papago left, the bird count at that oasis plummeted. Today, there are twice as many species at the still-inhabited oasis as at the now-deserted one. The species diversity and richness of habitat was dependent in this case on human interaction with the landscape.[10]

lower the consumption of building materials, thus protecting forests and endangered species.

AFFORDABILITY

If a house is cheaper to operate, it is more affordable. The reduced costs may make ownership possible for some individuals who might not otherwise be able to qualify for a mortgage. Many lenders are now required to consider projected utility bills as a factor in mortgage qualification. Energy Rated Homes of America, for example, provides ratings that banks and mortgage insurers, including the FHA and VA, can use to write "energy-efficient mortgages."[11] From the homeowner's perspective, it certainly makes more sense to spend hard-won income on a tax-deductible, equity-building mortgage than on perpetual utility bills.[12]

These same issues hold true for commercial buildings. The less money a business must spend on mortgages and utility bills, the more is available to pay off business loans, invest in capital improvements, increase inventories, or hire new employees.

PRODUCTIVITY

From an employer's standpoint, the strongest reason to build green has to do with worker productivity. This single benefit of green buildings is so dramatic that it alone is a compelling argument for their construction, as the chart on the following page shows.

The idea that human beings will be more productive in pleasing surroundings has an intuitive logic that has now been demonstrated scientifically. Several recent studies have shown that making a building environmentally responsive can increase worker productivity by 6% to 15% or more. Since a typical commercial employer spends about 70 times as much money on salaries as on energy, any increase in productivity can dramatically shorten a green building's payback period, while making a business much more profitable. Saving $1 per square foot in energy costs can have a significant effect on a building's financial performance, *but that saving is absolutely swamped by the benefit of keeping workers—employed at an average annual cost of at least $130 per square foot—happy and productive.*

Greenbacks in Osage

Sustainable development can serve as an economic catalyst for an entire community.[13] For example, an energy efficiency program started in 1974 by the municipal utility in Osage, Iowa (pop. 3,500) keeps an additional $1.5 million per year in the local economy. Relying on simple tools like caulk guns, duct tape, better insulation, and efficient light bulbs, the program keeps an equivalent of $750 to $1000 per household per year in the community—recirculating around Main Street, supporting local jobs and making Osage noticeably more prosperous than comparable towns nearby.[14]

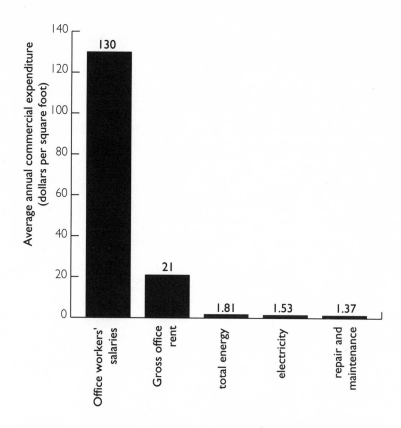

Data from Building Owners and Managers Association; Electric Power Research Institute; *Statistical Abstract of the United States 1991.*

A Primer on Sustainable Building

HUMAN HEALTH

If it's hard to work smart in a dumb building, it's also hard to stay healthy in a sick one. Although no one really knows what percentage of health problems are related to building ecology, there is little doubt that many work-related illnesses, headaches, and eyestrain are directly related to poor lighting, inadequate fresh air, harsh acoustics, and the gloomy surroundings that prevail in many office spaces. In several studies, when a company moved into a green building, absenteeism dropped by 15% to 25%, and sick-leave use was significantly reduced.[15] This suggests that such buildings are not just nicer; they are also healthier.

View of N M B

Workers like the combination of daylighting and efficient electric lighting that green buildings provide. They like the pleasing views. They like the fresh air. They like the calm—the absence of harsh noises produced by mechanical devices laboring to heat or cool a poorly designed structure. In short, they like being in a space designed with human beings in mind. Workers at NMB, the Netherlands bank, like their new offices so much that many spend more time in the building. Together, all these enhancements serve to increase worker morale, improve the quality of work performed, reduce mistakes, and raise productivity.[16]

While this information is especially relevant for employers, it is also important for homeowners and home builders. Families also benefit from the natural lighting, better ventilation, air quality, and comfort found in sustainable homes. The fact that such buildings are also easier to heat and cool contributes to this sense of well-being, as lower utility bills free up money for other uses.

A Primer on Sustainable Building

II. Green Building Design

"...When you build a thing you cannot merely build that thing in isolation, but must also repair the world about it, and within it...and the thing which you make takes its place in the web of nature."
—CHRISTOPHER ALEXANDER, ARCHITECT, 1977

The overall goal of green building design is quite simple: you want to design a wonderful building—a building that is bright and well-lit, that is warm in winter and cool in summer, that is as comfortable as it is healthy, that is energy- and resource-efficient, that is functional and long-lived, and that promotes the well-being of its occupants and the earth.

Before beginning the design work, consider these five principles: First, remember the importance of thorough planning. Sustainable design is front-loaded—the work comes at the beginning, the rewards later. Early decisions are in many ways the most important, so allow enough time for conceptual thinking. Do not "design in haste and repent at leisure."

Second, sustainable design is more a philosophy of building than a building style. Most energy efficiency and other green technologies are essentially "invisible"; that is, they can be blended into any architectural style. While green features can be highlighted to demonstrate a building's connection to the environment, they do not have to dominate the design.

Third, green buildings don't need to be inordinately expensive or complicated. Although environmental awareness or rapid paybacks from reduced operating expenses could justify spending more money for a sustainable building, that's usually not necessary. Indeed, there is no intrinsic reason why a $40,000 home should not be as green as an $800,000 mansion.

Fourth, an integrated approach is critically important. If you design a conventional building, *then* throw a laundry list of technologies at it, you're liable to end up with a piecemeal or "50 stupid things" approach—one that may cost more and perform slightly better than a conventional building. On the other hand, adopting this Primer's recommendations in a systematic manner will result in a more livable, economical building. An integrated approach may incur higher prices for some pieces in order to achieve larger savings for the whole. For example, you may spend more on better windows which will allow you to spend less on a smaller furnace. This will always result in lower operating costs; in many cases, it will lower capital costs too.

Finally, although a green building will be more than just energy-efficient, minimizing energy consumption is so central a goal that it should serve as an organizing principle. Thus, the various design elements of a green building fall into three broad categories: energy-saving architectural features; an energy-conserving building shell; and energy-efficient furnaces, air conditioners, water heaters, lights, and other appliances.

AN ANCIENT ART

"The true basis for the more serious study of the art of architecture lies with those indigenous humble buildings that are to architecture what folklore is to literature, or folksong to music..."
—FRANK LLOYD WRIGHT, ARCHITECT, ~ 1930

Anasazi ruins

In discussing green design, a bit of historical perspective is useful. It's important to understand that the idea is *not* new. For millennia, most buildings were of necessity sustainable. It is only in the past century or so, as cheap energy, large sheets of glass, and air conditioning appeared, that architecture lost its moorings and forgot the ancient truth that the most important building covenants are dictated by the earth. A building designed to heed its surroundings will naturally be more energy-efficient and will make elegant and frugal use of local materials.

If we modern Americans, who spend an average of 80% of our time indoors, wish to exist in harmony with our environment, we must do by choice what our ancestors did out of necessity—design with the climate and with a sense of place.

DOLLARS AND SENSE

"The bottom line of green is black."
—TEDD SAUNDERS, BUSINESSMAN, 1994

What does a green building cost to build? Sometimes a bit more, sometimes less, but in general it should cost about the same as a conventional one of the same size. However, a look at the bottom-line cost will not always reveal differences and cost-shifting within the green building's budget. Take windows, for example.

Efficient superwindows are more expensive than standard windows. However, installing superwindows can reduce heat gain in hot climates, net a higher heat gain in cold climates, and reduce lifetime energy costs. The reduction in unwanted heat flows allows you to downsize (or even eliminate) the heating and/or cooling system. A smaller heating, ventilating, and air conditioning (HVAC) system will cost less to buy, often enough less to immediately offset the additional price of the superwindows. Of course, the building will be far cheaper to run. In addition, superwindows cut noise, improve radiant comfort, and even eliminate perimeter zone heating in commercial buildings, saving floorspace. Altogether, they yield ten kinds of significant benefits, of which saved energy is only one.

Similarly, important indirect savings can result from using water-efficient toilets, showerheads, and faucets. Efficient hardware costs little, if anything, extra to buy, yet can save money on tap fees and septic-system sizing as well as giving you lower monthly water bills.

Note, however, that the full financial benefits will only accrue if you take an *integrated approach*. Installing superwindows without downsizing the HVAC, or high-performance toilets without reducing the leach-field size, will lower your operating costs, but will not allow savings on capital costs. It's far better to come out ahead in both the short *and* the long run.

Bottom line? In designing a green building, vigilantly root out waste and redundancies. Continually ask, "By doing this, what can be eliminated?" The art of green design is not just what is put into a building, but what is left *out*. The nicest systems are the ones you no longer need.

Trade-offs in the Audubon House

In a world where buildings are seen as products to be delivered "fast, cheap, and with a pretty face," the Audubon House has developed a new set of priorities. Although there are no marble lobbies, bronze handrails, or rare wood paneling, the building is quite beautiful, filled with natural light and "with an enhanced awareness of the time of day and season." The money usually invested in expensive finishes was instead "invested in people—in their comfort and well being." Natural daylighting, efficient lighting, and materials chosen to improve indoor air quality were used, "and the payback will be in enhanced productivity."[17]

A SENSE OF PLACE

"…we must at the outset take note of the countries and climates in
which buildings are built."
—VITRUVIUS, ARCHITECT, ~110 BC

The Bedouin Tent

The Bedouin tent accomplishes five things at once. In the desert, temperatures often exceed 120 degrees Fahrenheit. But the black tent creates a deep shade that brings the sensible temperature to 95 degrees. The weave is very coarse, which creates a beautifully illuminated interior. The coarse weave and the dark surface encourage the air inside to rise. The incoming breeze drops the temperature even lower, down to 90 degrees. When it rains, the fibers swell and the tent becomes waterproof. And of course, it can be rolled up and taken along when these nomadic people move.

Each region of the country has a traditional building form or "vernacular architecture." Since these styles embody a great deal of experience, wisdom, and cleverness, it's worth studying the layout, basic design, and orientation of older buildings in some detail for valuable clues and ideas. In particular, vernacular architecture is almost always climactically appropriate.

For example, the "dogtrot"-style homes found in the South are an ideal response to a hot, humid climate. But where the climate is hot and dry, the "courtyard" adobe found in New Mexico makes more

Bedouin tents

sense. In cloudy, cold New England, a compact "saltbox" design works well.

Incorporating suitable elements of vernacular design into a building will improve its energy efficiency and comfort. For example, adding adobe or other thermal mass to houses in the deserts of the Southwest can make them much easier to keep cool.

Depending on the climate, other features such as wide overhangs, airlock entries, arcades or porches, atria, and natural ventilation may boost the building's efficiency.

One aspect of vernacular architecture that is frequently overlooked is building color. Roof color, especially, may substantially affect a building's energy use. In a hot climate, a white or light-colored roof in combination with well-placed shade trees can lower the building's cooling load by 30%.[18] Another important aspect is the absorption of the infrared half of solar energy: some pastel finishes reflect infrared well, while some visually "white"-looking asphalt shingles absorb it.

SOLVING FOR PATTERN

"…you are on the right track when your solution for one problem accidentally solves several others. You decide to minimize automobile use to conserve fossil fuels, for example, and realize that this will reduce noise, conserve land by minimizing streets and parking, multiply opportunities for social contact, beautify the neighborhood and make it safer for children."
—MICHAEL CORBETT, DEVELOPER, 1984

Vernacular architecture works so well in large part because it "solves for pattern"—a key concept in sustainable design. The term, if not the concept, may be unfamiliar: it comes from an essay in which Wendell Berry—a Kentucky farmer, poet, and author—examines the nature of solutions, good and bad, found in American agriculture. Although Berry's focus is farming, many of his points are relevant to architecture. In his words, "They will serve the making of sewer systems or households as readily as they will serve the making of farms."

According to Berry, a good solution will:

- solve more than one problem, while not making new problems.

- satisfy a whole range of criteria; be good in all respects.

- accept given limits using, so far as possible, what is at hand.

- improve the balances, symmetries, or harmonies within a pattern.

If Berry's list seems ambitious, that's because it is. He is not looking for solutions "that solve problems by ignoring them, accepting them as trade-offs, or bequeathing them to posterity." But it should be noted that, although their criteria may not be as sweeping as Berry's, many architects and builders already solve for pattern, or attempt to, on every job. Examples of existing building materials, construction techniques, and design strategies that solve for pattern are numerous. Using low-e windows in conjunction with passive solar design cuts utility bills, makes rooms more comfortable at night, and reduces furniture fading.

Here's another example. Most housing developments deal with storm run-off by channeling it into concrete storm drains and then to a municipal sewage system. In big storms, the run-off overloads the treatment plant; the rainwater, now mixed with sewage, overflows into streams. A better alternative is a natural drainage system with surface swales, tiny check dams, and depressions that can serve as temporary retention ponds and percolation beds. By mimicking nature, this system produces beautiful landscaping, reduces off-site water flow, eliminates sewage-treatment concerns, and costs substantially less to build and maintain than conventional storm drainage. It solves for pattern.

A busy contractor trying to finish a building on time and within budget might not think she has time to solve for pattern. In order for your building or development to solve for pattern, the bulk of the work must be done up front, in the process of making fundamental decisions about the building's shape, size, orientation, and layout. Sometimes an ingenious solution can be jury-rigged at the last minute by a clever builder, but it's not wise to count on that. If you can't afford to do it right the first time, how can you afford to do it twice?

Drainage swales at village homes

GETTING STARTED

> *"Whatever you can do, or dream you can, begin it.*
> *Boldness has genius, power, and magic in it."*
> —GOETHE, POET, ~1820

If green buildings and green developments have so many advantages, why aren't more being built? It's not because they are more expensive; typically they aren't. And it's not because builders don't care about the environment; many do. But there are good reasons why green buildings still command just a sliver, albeit a steadily expanding one, of the building market. First and foremost, the field is still very new; word is just getting around. To talk of a "green" building five years ago, when many developments now coming on line were being planned, was to discuss which paint to use.

A second hurdle is posed by the logistical and time constraints that architects and builders face. All building projects are complicated due to permits, scheduling, weather, interest rates, lumber costs, and so on. With so many variables to consider and so many pitfalls to avoid, builders like to keep things as simple as they can. There's little room in the construction industry for anything suggestive of "experimentation."

A third concern is marketability. In the intensely competitive housing market, the safest path is the tried-and-true. In typical "Catch 22" fashion, some use the excuse that the "marketplace" is not interested in green buildings and we know that because no one is building them. However, if no one is offering such buildings, how can the marketplace respond? Those builders who take the risk are well rewarded, but if no one in a given area has tried it, few have the leverage or boldness to be the first. There is also a problem of incentives: many, although not all, of the financial and other benefits of green buildings accrue to the ultimate owner, rather than the builder or contractor. The bottom line is that building green is a new challenge for an industry that often feels challenged enough as it is.

We recognize that the green agenda is an ambitious one and that making the commitment to follow it can be intimidating. For now at least, sustainable buildings require more thought and planning than conventional construction. Additional lead time is needed to master the wealth of new information, design tools, ecological understanding, and building products that have recently become available.

How can you cost-effectively incorporate this new information? Perhaps the best way is to tackle the process incrementally. Before beginning a project, ask yourself how big a bite you can take. Can you tackle the issue of energy efficiency? Habitat protection? Selection of healthy building materials? Take on only as much as you are comfortable with. Learn from each project, then bite off a little bit more, do it better the next time, and steadily expand the scope and depth of your design integration.

Greenness isn't all or nothing, black or white. There's a *spectrum:* some buildings are better, some worse. A tract home being built today with its better insulation, windows, and appliances is much greener in some respects than one built twenty years ago. The indus-

On Accepting a New Challenge

Fifty years ago, as he organized the first Scottish expedition to the Himalayas, mountaineer W.H. Murray, quoting Goethe's work, wrote: "Concerning all acts of initiative (and creation), there is one elementary truth, the ignorance of which kills countless ideas and splendid plans: that is, the moment one definitely commits oneself, then Providence moves too. A whole stream of events issues from the decision, raising in one's favor all manner of…assistance, which no man could have dreamt would have come his way."

try *is* headed in the right direction.

The priorities you place on different aspects of green design will vary from job to job and client to client. The first step is simply making a commitment to minimize a project's overall environmental impact. A key issue for any building, and one of the easiest to address, is energy efficiency. Saving energy has a powerful multiplier effect. The aspect of green design that currently requires the most effort is probably the selection of green building materials. Right now, they are sometimes difficult to find and often cost more than conventional materials. The market, however, is changing rapidly and this will become easier.

To repeat, a building that is partly green is far better than one that's not. So, go as green as your time, skills, client, and project permit. If your decisions save some lumber, some energy, or some water, you're definitely doing the right thing. Next time, try even more.

III. Site Selection

*"What will this place require us to do? Permit us to do?
Help us to do?"*
—WENDELL BERRY, FARMER AND POET, 1992

Although site selection is an important issue in conventional construction, it is absolutely critical to the success of a sustainable building project. For this reason, green builders and architects must address many site issues that are traditionally ignored.

Bamberton, a new town proposed in British Columbia, is reusing an abandoned industrial site. Existing steel structures will form the downtown commercial core.

An ideal green development site would offer clean air, water, and soil; provide solar access and perhaps access to other forms of renewable energy; have public transportation nearby; be close to existing workplaces, schools, libraries, shopping centers, and other community services; utilize an existing infrastructure of roads and utilities; have the potential to be developed without causing undue environmental harm; and, in some cases, provide an opportunity to reuse or renovate existing structures.

Of course, "ideal" sites are rare. It is possible, while evaluating land, to be both practical and open-minded. Innovative solutions and unusual opportunities can be sought out. Many less-than-ideal sites can be enhanced by careful design and development; a creative builder or architect can often discover ingenious solutions that will minimize the site's shortcomings. In any case, since the site is a critical component—perhaps *the* critical component—in a green building project, questions about the land's appropriateness are crucial. The following checklist can help:

■ **Is the land suitable for development?** Just because it's for sale, don't presume that development is either desirable or inevitable. The first question to ask is, Should *anything* happen there? What is the site's "carrying capacity"? Can it be developed without being destroyed?[19]

*The presence of a rare species does not
always rule out development. Some sites
can be developed with appropriate
buffer zones; on others, thoughtful
development can actually create
additional habitat. In one case, a
project was planned for a site whose
open meadows were home to an
endangered butterfly. If the land had
been protected, ecological succession
would have transformed the meadows
into scrublands and the butterflies
would have disappeared. In this
example, by preserving the meadows,
the development served to benefit the
butterfly.[21]*

■ **Are there better uses for the site?** Think twice or perhaps three times before converting productive farmlands to housing or commercial buildings. If developing a rural site, can development be clustered and construction contained to preserve valuable agricultural lands or fragile ecosystems?

■ **Does the land have cultural, historical, or archeological significance?** Does it have a geographical link to an existing community? A desirable sense of place? If so, can that be preserved while developing the site?

■ **Is redevelopment possible?** In general, redeveloping an urban or suburban site will cause less harm than bulldozing a virgin one. Areas with an existing infrastructure of utilities, roads, and possibly mass transit are prime candidates for sustainable development.

■ **Are clean air, water, and soils present?** Is smog an issue? Has the site been contaminated in the past by agricultural, industrial, or urban pollution? Do nearby airports, industrial sites, and highways cast an acoustical or olfactory "shadow"? Before buying, it's a good idea to test the soils and proposed drinking water for contamination.[20]

■ **Does the site have solar access?** Green buildings rely heavily on the sun for heat and light. The sun's path and existing shadow patterns will determine how much solar heating and daylighting you can obtain. Check for tall buildings or trees that might obstruct the sun. If the electrical grid is more than one-quarter mile away, is it economical to rely on the sun, wind, or falling water for electrical power?

■ **Are mass transit, roads, highways, and other transportation options nearby?** The answer has tremendous economic and environmental ramifications. Are buses or trains available? Bike paths? If not, how far will people have to drive to work? School? Shop? How far is the hospital? Fire station? Airport?

■ **What are the site's natural values?** What wildlife, plants, and habitats are present? Do bald eagles nest there? Are wetlands present? If the site has been degraded by past human activity, could sensitive development help restore it? If the site is, say, five acres in size or larger, you may wish to map its plants and wildlife to preserve significant natural areas better.

■ **What about topography, geology, and hydrology?** Does the site lend itself to development? Can you get a road in? How steep is the slope? What happens to run-off? Are the soils strong and stable enough to build on? If you plan a septic system, what's the percolation rate? Is radon a problem? Flooding? Wildfire?

■ **Are strong electromagnetic fields (EMF) present?** Although the dangers of EMF remain the subject of heated debate and ongoing studies, it makes sense to avoid building within about 100 yards of power transmission lines, electrical transformers, and radio, television, and microwave installations.

■ **Can existing structures be reused?** One principle of sustainable design is that existing buildings should be saved, remodeled, or reused whenever possible. If such buildings are beyond repair, can materials from them be economically salvaged?

■ **And finally, how might future development on adjacent lands affect your project?** As difficult as this question can be to answer, it's still worth trying to predict whether future development will enhance or detract from your project. Among other issues, consider whether new development will affect your site's access to water, transportation, and solar gain, deplete clean air, and add to pollution, noise, and congestion.

On first reading, this lengthy checklist may be a bit daunting. But note that it simply expands on the evaluation process that almost all builders and homeowners already conduct. Also note that many issues raised are relevant only to larger developments.

An experienced architect or builder can make an initial assessment of a small site in a day or less. Granted, if you are unfamiliar with the local ecology, you may have to hire someone to help answer some of the questions raised, but even in that case a survey should not prove unduly expensive or time-consuming.

While the questions raised here can help answer concerns about the site under consideration or help you compare sites, you will eventually still need to decide what is most important for your building. Every site is different. Few are perfect. Use a creative design to make virtues out of what may at first appear to be failings.

In the end, though, the decision to buy or not to will often boil down to two points of intuition: Does the land feel right? Would you feel right developing it?

IV. SITE DEVELOPMENT

"Each hill had been bulldozed to fill a valley…every tree, shrub, marsh, rock fern and orchid, every single vestige of that which had been, was gone."
—IAN L. MCHARG, ECOLOGICAL PLANNER, 1969

The past practice of blindly clearing a building site with little if any regard for what's already there is no longer desirable or acceptable. As green builders and developers, we must rethink the relationships between the land and development. Realtors often speak of "raw land" or a "vacant lot." Both phrases imply that land is simply a *commodity* belonging to us. The truth is, land is a *community* to which we belong. If we want that community—and by extension, ourselves—to prosper, we must design with it in mind.

Almost fifty years ago, the noted ecologist Aldo Leopold wrote: "There is as yet no ethic dealing with man's relation to land and to the animals and plants which grow upon it…. The land-relation is still strictly economic, entailing privileges but not obligations." Leopold's call for a new "land ethic" is one of the cornerstones of green design. In truth, there are very few truly vacant lots; almost every tract of land supports some type of natural community of plants and animals whose expendability should not simply be taken for granted.

Sustainable design aims to cause minimal environmental harm. An overly ambitious ideal? Not necessarily. Although erecting a building or buildings will always cause some ecological disruption, it can be dramatically reduced, if not entirely eliminated, through restraint and careful planning. In the case of land whose productivity has been degraded by past human activity, green development can frequently restore environmental productivity and enhance biological diversity.

After locating a site for your sustainable development, carefully consider how it can best be used. Most sites can be developed in a variety of ways; you want to discover the one or two that are most harmonious and least injurious. For this, there's no substitute for spending time—lots of it—on the land. As you do, mull over the questions Wendell Berry poses: "What will this place require us to do? Permit us to do? Help us to do?"

Roads and Utilities

Called in to consult on a large gas pipeline routed through a forested park, Andropogon Associates, a Philadelphia-based landscape architecture firm, dramatically reduced construction damage by requiring that all earth-moving equipment work on top of the soil and that the pipe be welded in the trench. The forest floor was removed in large blocks—18 inches thick—using a specially modified front-end loader and reset as the pipeline progressed. The park was quickly restored, leaving no scars.[22]

As you begin to develop a preliminary design, take full advantage of whatever technical data you possess, but don't overlook human resources. Old-timers will often have priceless insights into the land and its possibilities. Base decisions on topography, environmental concerns, and infrastructure issues. Consider solar access, water run-off, and the local climate.

Always protect the site's natural resources. Wetlands, woodlands, trails, lakes, and streams are powerful amenities. Preserve them whenever possible. If a stream or marsh or wood lot has been degraded, consider restoring it. Before beginning, ask your neighbors and native people for advice and suggestions. In some cases, particularly with urban or suburban sites, there may be little growing there. If that's the case, make restoration a goal from the beginning.

Study and respect the site's manmade features in the same way you do its natural ones. If historic barns, houses, bridges, or other structures are present, try to save them. Incorporating examples of regional culture and vernacular building styles into your project will do much to enrich its character and give it a sense of place.

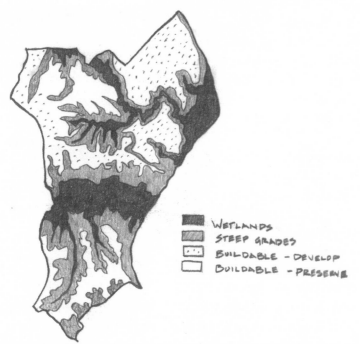

Developers of Haymount, a new project in northern Virginia, did extensive environmental mapping before deciding where to build. This diagram shows wetlands and other preserved areas.

When installing underground utilities and roads, strive to minimize damage. For a single-family home, the placement of the driveway is a critical decision with many hidden implications. In larger developments, the orientation of roads and platting of lots will have a tremendous effect—for better or worse—on what is built there. Water, sewer, and electric lines, gas lines, and other utilities should be unobtrusive; bury them if possible.

The developers of Dewees Island, a 1,206-acre retreat 12 miles northeast of Charleston, South Carolina, are trying to prove that man and nature can coexist in a harmonious balance. Over 65% of the island—780 acres—will be protected from any disturbance whatsoever; about half that has been designated a wildlife refuge. Houses will be clustered and are designed to "nest within the trees." Other nice features of the development include: No paved roads. No cars. No private docks. No golf course.

The developers have gone to great lengths to involve a broad cross-section of Charleston residents in design decisions. Members of the "Harmony Project" team include botanists, biologists, and other scientists, local politicians, building officials, architects, and schoolchildren. All are working together to preserve the island's environmental and cultural heritage. A small museum and library have been established. Area schoolchildren take field trips to the island to learn about its ecosystems and human history. A marine biologist and an environmentalist monitor the island's ecosystems. And an annual sweet-grass basket competition has helped revive a nearly forgotten tradition.[23]

A Primer on Sustainable Building

V. TRANSPORTATION

"Automobiles are often tagged as the villains responsible for the ills of the cities. But the destructive effects of automobiles are much less a cause than a symptom of our incompetence at city building."
—JANE JACOBS, AUTHOR, 1961

Americans love the mobility cars provide, but our reliance on them as the sole means of personal transport has had a hugely negative effect on the environment, on our social interactions, and, we would argue, on the building profession. Streets, parking lots, highways—the needs of automobiles—are literally a driving issue in every real estate project. Almost all residential and most commercial development in the United States is inherently unsustainable because it essentially requires people to own a car simply to get around.

The automobile's environmental impacts are widely recognized—from urban smog to global warming to oil spills in Alaska's Prince William Sound. Their impact on community is less obvious. Busy streets divide neighborhoods. Cars isolate one person from another. Traffic jams take a daily toll on commuters who each year spend more and more time shuttling to and from work. Finally, the absence of convenient transportation alternatives effectively strands the one-third of Americans too poor, young, old, or infirm to drive.

Cars also impose burdensome demands on developers. They must deal with questions of street placement and the need for costly new roads, curbs, highways, and parking areas, not to mention the architectural challenge of trying to blend a three-car garage into a house's façade.

For almost fifty years, subdivisions have been designed around the needs not of people but of cars. Now, as highway congestion grows and the myth of the open road wears thin, new patterns of development are emerging. Some developers are embracing "neotraditional planning" or "pedestrian pocket" designs that cluster development, reduce automobile traffic, promote walking and biking, and preserve natural spaces. Although such developments are not car-free, they do make it practical to get around without a car. Certainly, they are far more sustainable than the suburban sprawl we are accustomed to.

"It has lately been assumed that people no longer want to walk to local stores. This assumption is mistaken."
—FROM *A PATTERN LANGUAGE* BY CHRISTOPHER ALEXANDER

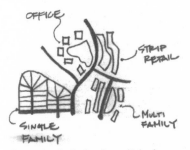
Conventional suburban "sprawl" development

Neo-traditional development

For green development, *making vehicular access the primary consideration is no longer desirable.* Even small developments can be designed with the pedestrian in mind. Something as simple as making streets narrower will "calm" traffic and enhance safety for pedestrians, drivers, and children.[24] Narrow streets have other advantages. Since they require less asphalt to pave, they are cheaper to construct. Rainwater run-off is diminished. Unwanted summer heat gain—the black-pavement effect—is reduced. Integrating narrow streets with pedestrian paths and bikeways promotes the almost lost amenity of walking. As people walk, they meet their neighbors and friends. The neighborhood comes alive. Dedicating less land to automobiles means that more is available for people, parks, and greenbelts. As they make streets narrower, developers should also reduce the size of parking lots. Where parking is needed, integrate it into the overall landscaping design. Many times, parking areas don't even need to be paved; new products allow them to be grass-covered. If the need for parking is strictly seasonal or for only part of the day, then the parking area can be designed for alternative uses, like a basketball court, during "off-hours."

Perhaps the real transportation problem is that too many of us live in a fractured universe. We sleep in one place, work in another, shop in a third. The old-style subdivision, dedicated solely to houses, reinforces this. A green subdivision combats it by providing a mix of houses, offices, shops, and schools so that residents can meet their needs and integrate their lives without a car.

Whenever possible, sustainable developments should be sited to take advantage of existing roads, highways, and public transit. By doing so you help link your new project to the existing community and reduce automobile dependence. The ease of integrating a new project into the existing transportation network will depend on its location. New subdivisions should also aim to promote walking, biking, and mass transit use. Whenever possible, individual homes and office buildings should also be located so that the occupants can take advantage of public transit.

Do not underestimate the economic importance of alternative transportation options. As demand for pedestrian-based communities increases, convenient access to buses, subways, trains, or light rail has been shown to increase significantly the value of a new development.

Home buyers (and, by extension, home builders) may soon be able to profit from so-called "no-car mortgages" that account for the real cost of owning and running an automobile, often $300 or more a month. If a new home is so located that it doesn't require you to own a car, that sum can be applied to a mortgage qualification instead.

Owners of green commercial buildings or the private companies that rent them can use parking "feebates" to encourage carpooling. Feebates are cash payments, or free transit passes, given to employees by their employers in lieu of free parking. Employers save money by leasing fewer parking spaces. In some communities, employers must meet stringent requirements to reduce employees' automobile use, and feebates are an economically viable solution that works. Employees benefit as well because they can pocket the difference between the costs of alternative means of access to work and their parking feebates.

Pedestrian Pocket

The developers of Laguna West, a subdivision near Sacramento, aim to "create an environment where homes, schools, work, and shops are all within easy walking distance…where it is as easy…to get around by foot or bike as with a car." Their plans for narrow streets were initially opposed by public works agencies who had concerns about access for garbage trucks and emergency vehicles.

According to Susan Baltake, a member of the development team, "Each agency has requirements for street width. They are additive, so suburban streets are typically wide enough to land a plane on. To demonstrate that the access fears were groundless, we built a mock demonstration street. We brought in trees and concrete barriers similar to those we wanted to use for in-street tree wells. We parked all of our employees' cars on the street. Then we rented an ambulance, garbage truck, and fire truck that could handle a seven-story fire. We drove them up and down, backed them in and out, filmed it on video. It cost about $5,000—but we got our approvals."[25]

VI. Building Placement

"I have spoken to thousands of architects, and when I ask, 'How many of you know how to find true South?' I rarely get a raised hand."
—William McDonough, Architect, 1993

Although the exact placement of buildings will vary from site to site, some considerations hold true for all. For example, a green building should always be sited to maximize its beneficial use of the sun and other renewable resources and to minimize its impact on the natural environment. On a rural site, this might mean searching the land for its most attractive micro-climate; on an urban one, it might mean carefully plotting shadow patterns from surrounding buildings to optimize the solar gain on yours.

After you understand the seasonal changes in solar gain, place the building to maximize its solar access or shading, depending on the climate. Note that this must be done at the very beginning of the design process to optimize passive solar heating, daylighting, and natural cooling. For optimal performance, heat-gaining spaces should face within 15 degrees of due south. In most parts of the U.S., simply making the building the right shape and pointing it in the right direction can cut total energy use by 30–40% at no extra cost.

Orienting the building to capture expansive views or to achieve privacy and security should be done in concert with siting for solar access. The recent development of "superwindows" that can gain more heat than they lose, even when facing poleward, provides flexibility in window placement. Careful placement of windows still remains an impor-

> "My prescription for a modern house: first a good site. Pick one that has features making for character...then build your house so you may still look from where you stood upon all that charmed you, and lose nothing of what you saw before the house was built, but see more."
> —Frank Lloyd Wright

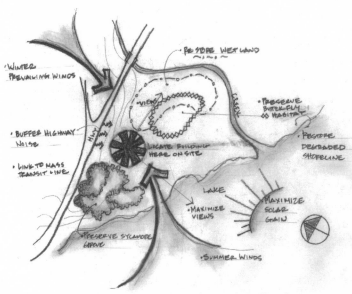

Considerations for building placement

tant consideration, however, particularly if the building is a passive solar one.

Take advantage of existing land-forms and vegetation to improve your building's energy performance and comfort. For example, earth berms can be used to provide shelter from blizzards or to deflect noise. Deciduous trees can block the hot summer sun while allowing solar gain in the winter.

Seasonal winds can have a significant effect on comfort, so orient the building to block winter gales and capture summer breezes. On a sloping site, it often makes the most sense to terrace the building with the existing grade, rather than bring in bulldozers to flatten the entire area. With developments, try to cluster buildings to preserve open space and wildlife habitat. This will also make it easier to keep roads and service lines short.

Finally, if there is one place on the site that is particularly beautiful, magical, or special, *don't build there.* Leave it alone, so that it always has the character that you love. All too often, buildings are placed on the best part of the site, and then the occupants wonder why the land has lost its magic. Building on the site's *least* interesting part is counter-intuitive, but a well-designed green building can make that place special as well.

VII. Land Design

"…all we need to live a good life lies about us. Sun, wind, people, buildings, stones, sea, birds, and plants surround us. Cooperation with all these things brings harmony."
—BILL MOLLISON, PERMACULTURE LEADER, 1991

Too often, the twin issues of open space and landscaping are addressed only after the site has been bulldozed or clear-cut and the building erected. Landscaping then becomes an expensive after-thought, a way to embellish or decorate the building. Open space is often neglected entirely; as "leftover land," it is too often viewed as worthless.

A better approach is to think ahead—to plan the landscape *before* you build. The imaginative use of open space in tandem with creative landscaping can be a powerful tool for keeping a building and its occupants in touch with nature. It can be used to connect the inside to the outside, to lure people into outdoor "rooms," to create mini-wild areas, and to maximize the building's energy performance.

Open Space

"Outdoor spaces which are merely 'left over' between buildings will, in general, not be used."
—CHRISTOPHER ALEXANDER, ARCHITECT, 1977

As you consider the site, plan the building's exterior spaces as carefully as you do its interior. In general, each portion of the open space should be designed with a specific activity or activities in mind—as a place to rest, stroll, read, eat, exercise, converse, make music, people-watch, or sun. Locate sitting and play areas adjacent to your buildings. Link these outdoor "rooms" with wide paths. Provide plenty of comfortable benches and chairs in both sunny and shaded areas—places that are open and sheltered. Make the open spaces "alive" and people will use them.

If several buildings are planned, site them carefully. The goal is to create "positive spaces" and enclosed areas between them.[26] Water—in fountains, small streams, or ponds—is one of the most powerful

Run-off and Rip-rap

The practice of channeling storm run-off from roofs and parking areas into sewage systems is not just outdated; it's expensive and harmful. A better approach is to capture run-off beneath "porous pavements" or in lakes and artificial marshes. Whatever you do, don't line existing streams with concrete or rip-rap to "protect the banks." Instead, use temporary retention ponds to slow the flow of water. Design them to drain in less than six days to prevent the hatching of mosquito larvae. Plant cattails, willows, and other water-loving plants in these places.

elements in landscape design. When designing open spaces, pay particular attention to natural drainage patterns. They can act as a design determinant and can produce beautiful landscaping features, serve as a wildlife habitat, reduce off-site water flow, supply water for landscaping, and cost substantially less to build and maintain than conventional storm drainage. These alternative systems use tiny check dams, surface swales, and depressions that serve as temporary retention ponds. On a site, they can save thousands of dollars, and citywide, billions.

LANDSCAPING

> *"Every site, particularly an urban one, should have some wilderness character. It's time to stop paving meadows and putting streams into culverts."*
> —LESLIE SAUER, LANDSCAPE ARCHITECT, 1990

As you lay out the building, examine the existing vegetation. Flag valuable trees and shrubs. Be sure the excavator knows which ones you want to save. Set up protective buffers around the drip-line; a mesh fence will do. If mature trees must be removed, consider transplanting them. In general, try to preserve as much vegetation as possible. This is especially important in urban sites and in arid or harsh climates where new plants are difficult to establish and slow to grow.

Select and place new plants carefully to blend with the existing ecosystem. Emphasize the use of native plants and those that are suited to the area's climate.

Shade trees can reduce ambient air temperature by 15°

This will benefit wildlife. In arid regions, design a water-efficient landscape or xeriscape.

Use new plantings in conjunction with existing vegetation to create a desirable micro-climate around your building. Shading the building and nearby paved surfaces from the summer sun can lower air temperature by as much as 15F°, significantly reducing the building's cooling load and energy consumption. Trees can also be used to block winter winds, control viewlines, and deflect unwanted noises.[27] Earthen berms can be used for the same purpose or to capture summer breezes.

If your landscaping options are limited by poor soil, use compost made from grass clippings and organic wastes produced in your building to boost soil fertility. Design to promote composting: provide an area for collecting it in the kitchen and for storing it outside. Where water is expensive or scarce, consider installing a graywater system to provide a source of nutrient-rich water for new plantings. Drip irrigation and automated sprinkler systems are cost-effective in many climates.

One aspect of landscaping that is too frequently overlooked is food production. Today, most food consumed in this country is grown with chemical fertilizers and biocides, freighted over long distances (averaging 1,300 miles), and then sold by huge supermarket chains. By some estimates, it now takes ten times as much energy to grow, ship, and process our food as the food itself contains. Apples from New Zealand and grapes from Chile look appealing on grocery shelves, but this energy-intensive agriculture is, in the long run, inherently unsustainable.

For this reason, a garden, orchard, cropland, or some other form of edible landscaping should be incorporated into almost every green building project. The home garden is more popular than ever. But edible landscaping can be used on commercial sites as well. To boost productivity, use organic, permaculture methods that blend fruit and nut trees, grapevines, and other edible plants and shrubs with ground crops.[28]

Gardens and edible landscaping are easily integrated into a landscape. For example, grapevines can be used to screen outdoor sitting areas. In addition to providing food, the vines become part of the cooling system. A built-in or detached greenhouse can extend the growing season, providing fresh, biocide-free vegetables during early spring and late fall. Of course, food production is not limited to plants. Indoor or outdoor fish ponds can also be incorporated into a landscape design. In some cases, a fish pond may even serve as the last step of a wastewater treatment system.

Known for its Produce

Almonds, grapes, nectarines, oranges, and other foods abound at Village Homes in Davis, California. Organic farming is conducted in the neighborhood's common areas. In some seasons, residents can choose their breakfast by seeing what is ripe on the branches. Produce from some of the community's gardens is sold to restaurants as far away as Berkeley and San Francisco. Income from the almond harvest is used to offset neighborhood association fees.[29]

Grapevines can provide summer shading and allow winter solar gain

A Primer on Sustainable Building

VIII. BUILDING CONFIGURATION

"We shape our dwellings, and afterwards our dwellings shape our lives."
—WINSTON CHURCHILL, PRIME MINISTER, 1960

A building's shape, interior layout, size, and solar orientation all affect its energy use and, by extension, its sustainability. For example, reducing a building's surface-to-volume ratio or getting its solar orientation right can reduce energy use by 30%. However, to maximize energy savings, all four variables must be considered in an integrated manner.

The following are some general guidelines on building shape. In cold climates, building form should be compact to reduce heat loss due to winter winds, and slightly elongated on the east-west axis to maximize solar gain. In temperate climates, where the goal is to maximize winter heat gain while minimizing summer overheating, the building should approximate an elongated rectangle running east-west. The length of roof overhangs for summer shading is a critical factor; the correct length will vary with climate and latitude.

In a hot and humid climate, heat gain through windows should be minimized and ventilation and shading maximized. The building form should typically be elongated on an axis perpendicular to summer winds and be open in plan. For hot and dry climates, solar gain should also be minimized through shading, especially on the western side. Air movement should be maximized with cross-ventilation. The building form should typically be slightly elongated on the east-west axis and u-shaped or have a courtyard.

A building's surface area is an important variable but often overlooked. Increasing the surface area by making the building taller or longer increases the rate of heat transfer. While this may be desirable in a warm climate to help cool the building, it is inefficient in a cold climate. If more surface area is needed for other reasons, such as daylighting, it may require extra insulation or other offsetting features.

Room Layout

The interior spaces of houses and office buildings should be planned to best meet the occupants' needs while optimizing energy performance. Those needs, of course, will vary widely from family to family and office to office. How best to meet them is the subject of countless books and magazines which can help guide a design. The following discussion is for the Northern Hemisphere.

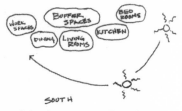

Orient living spaces to the south (in the Northern Hemisphere)

There's particularly good information on interior layout in both Alexander's *A Pattern Language* and Mazria's *The Passive Solar Energy Book*. These books were written with completely different approaches, but they end up with very similar recommendations. For example, Alexander's Pattern 128, "Indoor Sunlight," states, "Place the most important rooms along the south edge of the building, and spread the building out along the east-west axis. Fine-tune the arrangement so that the proper rooms are exposed to the southeast and the southwest sun. For example: give the common area a full southern exposure, bedrooms southeast, porch southwest. For most climates, this means the shape of the building is elongated east-west."

Alexander approaches the placement of rooms from the standpoint of how and when people use different spaces. Although Mazria's book approaches layout from the standpoint of solar heating, his recommendation is very similar and states, "Interior spaces can be supplied with much of their heating and lighting requirements by placing them along the south face of the building, thus capturing the sun's energy during different times of the day. Place rooms to the southeast, south, and southwest, according to their requirements for sunlight. Those spaces having minimal heating and lighting requirements, such as corridors, closets, laundry rooms, and garages, when placed along the north face of the building will serve as a buffer between the heated spaces and the colder north face."

Plan the layout of the kitchen carefully so that energy won't be wasted. For obvious reasons, don't put the refrigerator close to the oven. Spaces that generate net heat, like the kitchen, may do well on the north side if that fits the daylighting strategy and usage pattern. A little bit of common sense applied to the planning of interior spaces will go a long way toward making a building more energy-efficient.

In terms of window placement for lighting and ventilation, Alexander's Pattern 159, "Light on Two Sides of Every Room," states, "When they have a choice, people will always gravitate to those rooms which have light on two sides…," while Mazria's book states, "Locate [window] openings to admit sunlight and provide for ventilation…."

These recommendations focus on homes but are equally relevant for thinking about commercial spaces. For example, in the Audubon Headquarters, office spaces are on the outer walls, while meeting spaces, kitchens, and services areas are placed at the core. This was done to maximize daylighting and in response to the amount of time that spaces are occupied.

BUILDING SIZE

"Small rooms or dwellings discipline the mind, large ones weaken it."
—LEONARDO DA VINCI, ARTIST AND SCIENTIST, ~1500

In Aspen, Colorado, the Saudi Ambassador to the U.S., Prince Bandar bin Sultan ibu Abdul Aziz, built a 55,000-square-foot home. It covers more than an acre. Some members of the community were outraged. Next door, he built a much smaller guest cottage; the Prince prefers to stay in the cottage.

Appropriate building size—like other issues of scale—is rarely discussed in the United States. Many Americans are enthralled with large houses. Our cultural assumption is that we should buy as much house as we can afford. In the last five years, the average new house has increased in size by 10%. Almost one-third of new homes have four or more bedrooms; 76% have a two-car or larger garage. These trends would make sense if family size were increasing, but it's not. In fact, a third of U.S. households now consist of just one person. People are marrying later and having fewer children. Budgets are strapped. These changes argue for smaller, smarter houses, not larger, more wasteful ones.

As a rule, a green home or office building should be as big as it needs to be, but no bigger. The larger a building, the larger its environmental impact. Bigger buildings require more land, more lumber, more energy. Since architects and home builders typically make more money on larger homes, they have no incentive to encourage their clients and customers to build smaller. But does your client with two small children really need 4,000 square feet? Six bedrooms? Five bathrooms? Have they considered their energy bills? Property taxes?

Thoreau's famous cabin at Walden Pond was 10 x 15 feet—150 square feet.[30] Granted, he was a bachelor. During the thirteen years it took Thomas Jefferson to finish Monticello, his famous home in Virginia, he and his wife lived in a 210-square-foot brick cottage. As recently as 1950, when family sizes were much larger, homes in this country typically ranged between 800 and 1600 square feet.

The feeling of spaciousness is relative. For a Japanese family accustomed to 700 or 800 square feet, a 2,000-square-foot American home would be palatial. Although reasonable people can disagree about how big houses should be, beyond a certain point, bigness adds little and begins to subtract.

Smaller houses require fewer materials, less land, and less energy. Their prices are lower. Environmental consciousness is built-in. A small family can live perfectly well in a house of 1500 square feet or even smaller. Two McGill University architecture professors, Avi Friedman and Witold Rybczynski, attracted international attention after building a 1000-square-foot model house that is just 14 feet wide. "That's narrow for a house, but it is not narrow for a room, and for an eat-in kitchen 14 feet square is spacious," Rybczynski says. Hundreds of such homes have been sold in the Montréal area.

In New Haven, Connecticut, architect Melanie Taylor sells floor plans as small as 575 square feet. In her words: "Even people who can have whatever they want are doing this," she said. "People have tired of playing the 'whoever has the most toys wins' game." The "trophy home" era is not over, but as environmental awareness increases, the market for smaller, smarter, greener houses seems destined to grow.

SOLAR ORIENTATION AND DAYLIGHTING

"Light, God's eldest daughter, is a principal beauty in a building."
—THOMAS FULLER, THEOLOGIAN, 1642

In a conventional suburb, a house will face the street—regardless of which way the street runs. In rural areas, houses most often face the best view—regardless of which direction the view lies. Both practices severely constrain the opportunity to use the sun for passive solar heating or daylighting. In effect, they condemn many buildings to be darker, gloomier, and colder than they have to be.

Making the best use of the sun's heat and light is a central principle in green design. In some climates, the sun's heat is not needed. Then it becomes important to utilize the various techniques for passive cooling. Regardless of climate, all green buildings place an emphasis on using as much daylight as possible. Daylit buildings use substantially less energy while providing a welcome connection to the outdoors. Natural daylighting contributes to reduced operating costs, increased worker productivity, and the health and well-being of occupants. It also provides a superior quality of light.

There are many ways to get light deep into a building other than through windows and skylights; they include light monitors, clerestories, lightshelves, atria, courtyards, glass or glass-block or glass-topped partitions, top-silvering of venetian blinds (to bounce light off ceilings), and light-colored paints and furnishings.

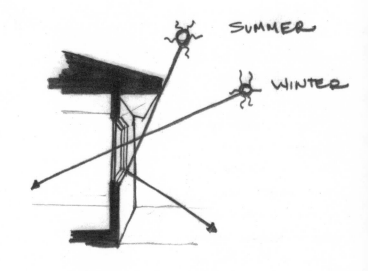

An example of a calculated overhang

A lightshelf, for example, is a white or reflective horizontal shelf mounted along exterior windows both inside and outside a building. It can be mounted below the window sill or at the top, above head-height. Lightshelves reduce window glare and bounce light upwards so it can reach deep into the interior. Light monitors, placed at the roof apex, are similar to skylights but better, because they control the quality and quantity of sunlight received. Whatever the design, careful attention to light distribution and brightness ratios is essential. Inexpert daylighting can cause glare and discomfort. It's easy to dump daylight into a space, but the point is putting it just in the right places at the right times.

An example of a light shelf that indirectly bathes the interior in glare-free natural light while shading the view glass from direct glare.

Daylit in Maryland

The Way Station, a 30,000-square-foot treatment center for the mentally ill in Frederick, Maryland, is heated and daylit with blend of windows, lightshelves, lightscoops, and skylights. Gathering places and offices flank a two-story courtyard that extends the full width of the building. Some skylights are equipped with Soluminaires—solar-powered reflectors that automatically adjust position. These and other efficiency measures decrease the building's energy consumption to one-third of normal.[31] Perhaps more important is the effect on the patients, who say, "There are no dark corners in the building." The architect notes that this may be especially relevant "for people who are already troubled with dark shadows within their minds."

IX. THE BUILDING SHELL

"Each year in the U.S. about $13 billion worth of energy—in the form of heated or cooled air—or $150 per household escapes through holes and cracks in residential buildings."
—AMERICAN COUNCIL FOR AN ENERGY-EFFICIENT ECONOMY

The building shell or envelope—its walls, windows, doors, and roof—should be designed to optimize thermal performance. Heat transfer through the shell occurs in three ways: conduction, infiltration, and radiation. In general, the shell should be designed to minimize conduction losses and the infiltration of hot air in the summer and the radiation of heated air in the winter. This general approach must obviously be applied to specific buildings according to their use, context, and climate. For example, airlock entryways make good sense in harsh climates. In any event, *all of the individual components of the building shell must be designed to work together as a system.*

The issue of insulation is a high-profile one. All builders and architects are by now familiar with general insulation principles and the R-values required by code in their climate. Building codes have great merit, but the insulation levels they require should be regarded as *floors*, not *ceilings*. (Bragging about a building's ability to "meet the codes" is really an admission that "if it were built any worse, it would be illegal."[32])

In many parts of the country, superinsulation is cost-effective to lower winter heat loss or summer cooling loads or both. The *type* of insulation used is not really an

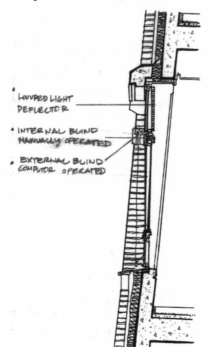

LOUVRED LIGHT DEFLECTOR

INTERNAL BLIND MANUALLY OPERATED

EXTERNAL BLIND COMPUTER OPERATED

Example of a wall section from N M B

issue for thermal performance, but the *amount* is. We recommend that the insulation specifications for green buildings be compared at a minimum to California's Title 24 requirements, the toughest in the country, not your local building codes. To be really sustainable, your building should probably beat the California standards: often the amount of insulation that minimizes construction cost, let alone life-cycle costs, is enough to eliminate heating and cooling systems. In an integrated design, insulation should also be considered in terms of its impact on indoor air quality and resource use.[33]

Some specific technologies may be appropriate in different climates. For example, in hot climates, installing a radiant barrier can boost a building's energy performance. The radiant barrier is an aluminized plastic film installed above the insulation and below the roof with the shiny side facing down. This thin film reflects radiant heat and can reduce cooling loads by 7% to 15%.[34] It may also slightly reduce heating loads.

WINDOWS

"I hummed the song and wiped the condensation from my giant picture window...so I could finally view the water. On the other side of the hermetically sealed glass, a gentle breeze swayed the palm trees, but I could not feel it. My picture window was bonded to the cinderblock walls. There were no sliding glass doors or small vent windows and seeing my breath frost up in the overly air-conditioned room with no thermostat, I knew that I was being protected from hurling myself to my death....(in a) three-foot plunge to the soft sand beach."
—JIMMY BUFFETT, SINGER, 1989

The biggest breakthrough in green building products over the past decade is the invention of better windows. Windows and other glazing materials are a critical component of the thermal envelope, daylighting system, and ventilation system. But until recently they were a mixed blessing: they let in light, but lost too much heat in winter and gained too much in summer. Even today, twice as much energy is lost through U.S. windows each year as flows through the Trans-Alaska pipeline. The introduction of "superwindows" with high insulating value and light transmittance marks a dramatic improvement.

Builder Guide

It is useful to be able to estimate how much energy a structure will consume and for what prior to construction. A number of computer software programs can help you do this. One is Builder Guide, available from the Passive Solar Industries Council. It runs on IBM-compatible computers and can be used to analyze single-family, multifamily, and small commercial buildings.[35] More elaborate models are a vital tool in optimizing the design of large buildings.

The term "superwindows" refers to double- or triple-paned windows filled with argon or krypton gas and containing an almost invisible "low-emissivity" coating. The low-e coating can be on the inner surface of one glass pane or on film (or films) suspended between two. The glass/film combination allows short-wave radiation (visible light) to enter while preventing long-wave radiation (infrared or heat) from entering or leaving. These glazings (also available in skylights and doors) offer R-values of 4.5 to nearly 12, compared to 1.7-1.9 for standard double-panes.[36] What's more, superwindows, which are offered by most window manufacturers, come in myriad different "flavors" for different climates. You can select one model to let in lots of light with little heat in Phoenix, or another to provide a net heat gain in Buffalo—*even in midwinter, facing due north.*

Although superwindows cost 15-50% more than standard double-panes, they make sense in both hot and cold climates everywhere, except on occasion in very mild climates where unwanted heat gain can be blocked more cheaply by proper placement of such shading as deciduous landscaping. Superwindows save lots of heating and cooling energy which makes it possible to downsize (or even eliminate) the furnace and air conditioner in residential buildings and the perimeter-zone heating in commercial buildings. It bears repeating that the new windows also block noise, increase comfort, and protect furnishings from ultraviolet damage.

Superwindows

Green Homes in Canada

The typical Canadian house built in the late 1970s used about 70,000 BTU per square foot per year. Homes built in the 1980s to meet the higher insulation standards of the government's R-2000 program use 33,600 BTU, or about half as much. The next-generation superinsulated "Advanced Houses" are projected to cut that in half again to about 16,800 BTU. These homes feature improved glazings, integrated space heating, cooling, and ventilation, and solar hot water.

The number and type of windows in a building should balance the need for daylight and heat with the need to minimize infiltration. In both commercial buildings and residences, windows should be positioned to capture views, provide ventilation, and meet daylighting requirements. It is desirable to specify different spectral characteristics—heat gain, emissivity, and transmittance—for different solar aspects. In other words, a north-facing window will be a different glass package than a south-facing window, a south-facing one may differ from a west-facing one, and so forth. If different windows "tuned" to each elevation can't be chosen, use a glazing with a low "shading coefficient" to prevent overheating on west and perhaps on south elevations.

In general, every room in a home or office should have at least one operable window. Operable windows are an essential element of passive cooling strategies that emphasize cross-ventilation. A fresh breeze, a birdsong, the smell of flowers—as well as the psychological benefits that operable windows provide—are significant. Studies show that people are happier across a much greater temperature range if they have the option of cranking their window open or shut.

Sometimes, however, open windows can cause problems. For example, if air pollution outside is high, then dirt, odors, and other contaminants can enter the building. Humidity can also be an issue. In cases where open windows might cause problems, good mechanical ventilation systems and filters may be necessary. Some designers prefer to combine fixed windows with operable *vents* that cost less, work well, need little maintenance, and can control rain, wind, insects, dust, and noise.

Many utilities offer rebates to encourage customers to install high-performance windows and glazings. Check with local utilities for more information. And, don't be misled by obsolete incentive structures that may reward a minimum shading coefficient even at the cost of blocking desired light as well as unwanted heat. A far better "figure of merit" is visible transmittance divided by shading coefficient—*i.e.*, ability to let in light while rejecting heat.

The Importance of a View

In the 1970s, a surgeon in Texas noticed that half his patients seemed to be getting well faster than the others. He noticed that the quicker-healing patients were also taking fewer strong painkillers and calling for the nurses less. The surgeon checked the patients' rooms and found that the faster-healing patients had windows that looked out on to trees. The slower-healing patients also had windows—but they faced a brick wall.[37]

BUILDING MATERIALS

"…our villages and towns were built from what came closest to hand: stone in Northamptonshire, timber in Herefordshire, cob in Devon, flint in the Sussex downs, brick in Nottinghamshire. Each town and each village has a different hue, a different feel, and fosters a fierce loyalty in those who belong there."
—HRH CHARLES, PRINCE OF WALES, 1989

From aluminum to zebrawood, literally hundreds of different materials can be used in a new building or the retrofit of an existing one. The conventional selection criteria are strength, cost, appearance, and suitability. To these, the green builder adds environmental impact, durability, and toxicity.

A wide range of green (or at least greener) building materials responds to one or more of these concerns. Although they can sometimes be hard to find, more environmentally responsible lumber, plywood, paints and finishes, fabrics, construction adhesives, insulation, and roof systems are all on the market. Some of these have been sustainably harvested. Some make efficient use of what once were considered "trash trees." Some have been salvaged. Some are formulated to reduce indoor air pollution. And some are products made from recycled glass, newspaper, plastic, tires, and other materials. Although green products are sometimes more expensive than their conventional counterparts, the gap is shrinking.

Wood has long been recognized as a wonderful building material whose primary shortcoming is the impact its harvest sometimes has on forests. With U.S. demand for lumber expected to reach 46 billion board feet in 1994, it's good practice to buy lumber from a company that cuts trees sustainably, replants afterwards, and strives to protect *forests*—which are very different from rows of identical *trees*. When possible, specifying wood products from operations certified as sustainable can minimize the use of old-growth lumber. Patronizing local sawmills, if they harvest sustainably, will also help.

Many engineered wood products, including laminated veneer lumbers (micro-lams) and wood panels (waferboard), that have come to market in the last two decades make economical use of lower-quality trees. Engineered lumber uses young, small-diameter, fast-growing

Building Materials

A typical American 1,700-square-foot new home will contain, among other things,[38]

- *9,700 board feet of lumber*
- *4,850 square feet of sheathing*
- *55 cubic yards of concrete*
- *2,528 square feet of siding*
- *2,000 square feet of shingles*
- *2,500 square feet of insulation*
- *6,484 square feet of drywall*
- *300 pounds of nails*
- *750 feet of copper wire*
- *280 feet of copper pipe*
- *170 feet of plastic pipe*
- *55 gallons of paint*

trees—wood that doesn't grow strong enough, straight enough, or big enough for large-dimension structural framing. Often, these products are stronger and lighter than the solid lumber they replace. For example, framing a floor with engineered wooden I-beams (such as those made by Trus Joist MacMillan) uses two to three times less wood than using Douglas fir 2x10s. Such an engineered wall can cut wood use almost fourfold, double insulation, increase strength, and reduce cost.

A material's durability, as measured in its life-cycle cost, has profound environmental ramifications. In many cases, the production and disposal of building materials has far worse consequences than the material's actual use. Extending the useful lifetime then becomes critical.

The toxicity of building materials has long been an issue both for the workers who use them and the occupants who must live with such materials. Asbestos. Lead solder. Oil-based paints. Formaldehyde-based glues. Pesticide-laced lumber. Volatile organic compounds (VOCs) given off by construction adhesives. Many building products are known to be toxic to some degree. For others (fiberglass insulation being one example), the jury is still out. Although asbestos, lead-based paint, and some other offenders have been removed from the market, it is wise to substitute green products for materials suspected of being hazardous. (The issue of indoor air quality is dealt with at greater length in Building Ecology, p. 83.)

When choosing building materials, prioritize the issues that are important to the project and the client. Remember that such products as plaster, linoleum, and cork have always been formulated in a way that is more environmentally friendly than some modern substitutes. Keep the adage "reduce, reuse, recycle" in mind:

■ **Reduce:** A smaller and/or more efficient building will require less concrete, fewer studs, less plywood, fewer gallons of paint, etc.

■ **Reuse:** Reusing building materials or, better yet, reusing a complete building reduces the amount of new materials needed. Of course, you should exercise caution when using salvaged materials. Be sure that they have an adequate efficiency performance and do not pose health problems. For example, don't install single-paned windows on exterior walls. Check wood products for lead-based paints.

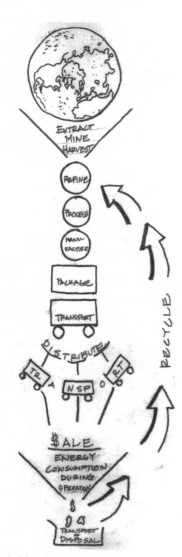

The life-cycle of a material

■ **Recycle:** Minimize your own waste through jobsite recycling. Construction sites are infamous for generating mounds of trash. Lumber offcuts, soda cans, empty boxes, plastic wrap, caulk tubes, joint compound and paint buckets, flashing scraps, sheetrock, pallets, roofing paper, cement bags, beer cans…the list goes on. Common practice is to burn anything that will burn and haul the rest to the dump. But some of this waste can be recycled. Depending on your location, aluminum flashing and cans, copper pipe, some kinds of plastic, cardboard, left-over paint, housewrap, and sheetrock can all be recycled and wood scraps may be reusable.

ENVIRONMENTAL IMPACT

"The original design for Wal-Mart's Eco-Store called for steel framing which requires nine times more energy to make and transport than does wood framing. A switch to wood saved thousands of gallons of oil in the fabrication of the building."
—WILLIAM MCDONOUGH, ARCHITECT, 1993

Historically, the construction industry has paid far more attention to the price of a building material than to the amount of energy needed to produce it. But while the "embodied energy" contained in building materials seems to be an esoteric concern, it too represents a price—in this case, one paid by the environment.

Embodied energy is the energy needed to grow, harvest, extract, manufacture, or otherwise produce a building product. Exact calculations are difficult, but one estimate of the relative energy intensity of various materials is: lumber = 1; brick = 2; cement = 2; glass = 3; fiberglass = 7; steel = 8; plastic = 30; and aluminum = 80.[39] Note that these figures are by *weight*. In other words, a pound of aluminum contains roughly 80 times as much embodied energy as a pound of wood. Volume comparisons obviously differ. Also note that these figures do not account for energy added during transportation. Adobe has very low embodied energy, but if it has to be shipped 400 miles, this virtue is negligible. Finally, these figures assume no recycling, which can save, for example, most of the energy on certain plastics and up to 95% for aluminum.

A Time-honored Bribe

One architect who wanted to sort and recycle construction waste met resistance from the construction workers. He motivated the crew in a time-honored fashion—with beer. On Fridays, he showed up with a case. If the recyclables had been sorted, the carpenters got the beer; if not, they didn't. After the first time the architect left without giving the construction crew the beer, the recyclables were sorted every time.

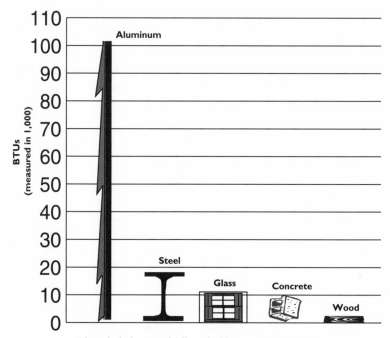

The embodied energy of different building materials in Btu/lb.

Lumber is low in embodied energy because it is made through photosynthesis, not with fossil fuels. The manufacture of steel, plastic, and aluminum requires increasing quantities of energy, so their negative impacts (measured in pollution, greenhouse gas production, and so forth) are greater. It is possible to minimize these costs by using materials that have low embodied energy, that are locally produced, and that will prove durable.

In the same way that it's often preferable to use wood studs rather than steel ones, it's better to use locally produced lumber, stone, cement, and plaster if available. This will lower the embodied energy of your project and help support the local economy. When importing a material, buy it from the *closest* source. If in New Hampshire, buy marble from Vermont rather than Italy.

The embodied energy of any material is only *one* measure of its environmental impact. Another is life-cycle analysis. In addition to a material's embodied energy, life-cycle analysis compares a product's life-span, durability, and structural efficiency. Since the manufacture of many building products is energy-intensive, a durable material that will last much longer than a less sturdy one will generally provide a net energy saving even if its embodied energy is greater. While steel beams have relatively high embodied energy, their strength, efficiency, and durability may make them a better choice in some applications than wooden beams. Life-cycle analysis argues for maximizing the *entire* building's longevity. Buildings shouldn't be thought of as disposable products. Instead of the customary 30-year design life, why not aim for a century or more? A green building can be an heirloom, a legacy, a gift to the future.

If a building is to have a long life, design it with flexibility in mind. For example, extending electrical wires and plumbing lines so that part of a house can be converted someday into a small apartment is easy to do. The same principle holds true for larger buildings. Wal-Mart's Eco-Mart in Lawrence, Kansas was designed so that it can be converted to housing after the building's retail life is over. Likewise, materials should be chosen for ease of reuse and disassembly. Are components created in such a way that they can easily be removed? Mercedes has learned that designing cars for ease of disassembly and recycling tends to lead to cars that are easier to assemble. Designing entire buildings that can have another use at the end of their original life need not mean featureless boxes with undifferentiated interiors. Sometimes, as in the Wal-Mart example, it may just involve a structural system that is sturdy enough to accommodate other uses. Stewart Brand, author of *How Buildings Learn*, says that all buildings are predictions, and ultimately all predictions are wrong. The issue now becomes how to design so that buildings can evolve gracefully.

No single analysis can give a definitive answer about whether to use a certain material. For example, fluorescent lamps use much less energy than incandescent lamps, but what about their toxic mercury content?[41] Life-cycle analysis does provide valuable information to help make informed choices, but it is not the final answer. In fact, a dogmatic position like "I will not use petrochemical products" may make you miss opportunities to optimize system performance. Remember to consider all the issues, including life-cycle costing, to ensure the best overall choice for the environment and the building.

The Question about Life-cycle Analysis

You may have questions about the "appropriateness" of using a material in a building because of its environmental performance. For example, should aluminum be used, with one of the highest amounts of embodied energy and with the damage bauxite mining does to the environment? Understanding these issues is complicated by the plethora of information available and by the emergence of "tactical research." The muddied debate can result from sponsored research (which may or may not subtly influence a report's conclusions) and easily manipulated computer models. It is increasingly possible to support or oppose just about any argument.[40] References like the American Institute of Architects' Environmental Resource Guide can help you find dispassionate guidance.

RETROFITS

"By retrofitting a 100-year-old building, rather than erect a new one, the National Audubon Society saved $9 million in construction costs. The retrofit also "saved" 300 tons of steel, 9,000 tons of masonry, and 560 tons of concrete."
—RANDOLPH R. CROXTON, ARCHITECT, 1993

The Lindbergh Crate

In 1927, after Charles Lindbergh's flight across the Atlantic, his plane was returned to the U.S. in a tongue-and-groove pine crate. With Lindbergh's permission, Vice Admiral Guy Burrage moved the crate to New Hampshire and converted it into a summer cottage. In 1962, the cottage was moved to a new spot. In 1990, nearing collapse, the crate/cottage was rescued for a third time and moved to Canaan, Maine. Lovingly restored, it is now a museum of Lindbergh memorabilia.[42]

Whenever possible, retrofit an old building's shell rather than demolishing it. Since the embodied energy in an existing building is large, its reuse will save much of the energy and expense of new construction, while eliminating demolition and disposal costs. In many cases, older buildings have wonderful architectural character that could not be cost-effectively replicated. What's more, they are often supported by an existing infrastructure and transportation system. Finding a new use for an old structure will also give a boost to the area's economy. If for some reason a sound building must be demolished, try to find someone who will move it to a new site or at least salvage the useful materials it contains.

In general, existing buildings should be retrofitted in accordance with the principles outlined here for constructing new ones. For commercial buildings, the priorities depend on whether the retrofit is an exhaustive one to be conducted all at once, or whether it will occur in phases.

If the building has been gutted and is to retrofitted all at once, first add insulation and superwindows. Second, install energy-efficient lighting and office equipment, along with water-saving plumbing fixtures. In most cases, this will allow downsizing of the heating, ventilation, and air conditioning (HVAC) systems. Well-designed retrofits can bring unexpected environmental and safety benefits. Lighting retrofits should replace pre-1978 ballasts (which can contain toxic PCBs) before they fail and perhaps leak, which can turn the ceiling and possibly the ventilating system into a toxic waste site whose clean-up may cost more than the building originally cost. If there's asbestos above the dropped ceiling, lighting retrofits can often work around it without disturbance.

If, however, the building is to be retrofitted space by space over time, improve the lighting and plumbing fixtures first; replace wasteful appliances and office equipment next; and upgrade the HVAC and building shell last.

Whatever the schedule, remember that energy-efficiency measures that may not seem attractive *individually* may be very attractive *in combination.* The wisdom of a systems approach is illustrated by the Audubon headquarters mentioned above. One of the most efficient office spaces in Manhattan, the building saves an estimated $78,000 per year in energy costs—not with fancy, high-tech energy systems, but with off-the-shelf materials used in integrated fashion.

Audubon House

According to architect Randolph Croxton, "Nothing in the building is cutting edge. It is simply a breakthrough in applied technology; its efficiency is achieved through a careful *layering* of conventional technologies in such a way that you get a powerful *cumulative* effect."

The best strategy for retrofitting a house is usually to make less expensive changes first. Tighten up the building envelope and reduce resource consumption with efficient lighting and water fixtures. Then use the resultant savings to pay for more expensive measures. (This presumes you aren't gutting the house. If you are, adopt the priorities outlined above for office buildings.)

In all retrofits, make every effort to avoid "cream-skimming"—undertaking retrofit measures one by one, in piecemeal fashion, in a way that reduces the total energy savings achieved. For example, installing an energy management system (EMS) in an old, inefficient building can yield savings of 20% to 25%. However, since the building itself remains inefficient, the EMS will have to be larger and more expensive than is really necessary. Once it's been installed, though, the lower energy bills may make it difficult to justify a more complete retrofit of lighting, heating, ventilation, and air conditioning systems. If, on the other hand, the lighting and HVAC systems are improved *first*, then you can buy a smaller and cheaper EMS. This integrated approach will cut the building's energy consumption by 50% or more.[43]

Among the most profitable buildings to retrofit are those whose glazing or mechanical systems need replacement because of age (or, in the case of mechanicals, because of the need to replace CFCs). In several recently analyzed cases, replacing these aging building elements with superwindows and super-efficient mechanicals—downsized by improved light and plug loads—has turned out to cost about the same as mere like-for-like replacement; yet it can save most of the energy while greatly improving amenity.

ALTERNATIVE CONSTRUCTION

> *"At the present rate of deforestation, tropical forests will be gone by the middle of the next century."*
> —AIA ENVIRONMENTAL RESOURCE GUIDE, 1992

There are many alternatives to conventional wood-framed or concrete-block construction that owner-builders might want to consider, either because they may be cheaper or because they use less wood and other resources. Among the alternatives are three ancient methods—adobe, native stone, and rammed earth—and a host of newer ideas, including waferboard-and-foam stressed-skin panels, concrete foam forms, underground or earth-sheltered homes, and even homes built out of straw bales or old tires.

Alternative building methods tend to come and go (remember geodesic domes?) because they sometimes work better in theory than in practice. (In theory, theory and practice are the same, but in practice, they're not.) Before proceeding, carefully consider their full implications. Adobe, rammed earth, stone, stressed-skin panels, and concrete-foam forms are all tried-and-true and can be used with confidence. Some of the newer ideas, however, are not fully proven.

Consider, for example, earth-bermed homes built of old tires and aluminum cans. These so-called "earthships" have been eloquently promoted by New Mexico architect Michael Reynolds. While these homes have good thermal performance, some aspects of the technique are problematic. For example, the tires, made of complex petro-

From the Ground Up

An owner-built home in Carbondale, Colorado used adobe-sized rammed-earth blocks. The dirt for the blocks was excavated onsite from the low-cost rubble-trench foundation. The walls were covered with rigid insulation outside and stuccoed. Inside, they were plastered. The mass acts as a thermal buffer. When outdoor temperatures drop to -20˚F, indoor air temperatures fall less than five degrees overnight.

chemicals, can emit gaseous compounds into the living spaces. Then there is the question of sealing aluminum into a wall. Aluminum is very high in embodied energy (as are tires), and probably should be recycled rather than buried. Finally, the construction method is basically rammed-earth, done one tire at a time. It is extremely labor-intensive, and unless you are very strong or have cheap help, such a structure is likely to be relatively expensive to build. Standard rammed-earth is easier.

A better alternative building material may be straw bales. Though reminiscent of the *Three Little Pigs*, the use of straw bales in construction has both a long history and positive implications for the environment. The first bale houses in this country were built more than a century ago on the Great Plains. Some still stand. The bales themselves are made of waste straw (with very low embodied energy) that would otherwise be burned, polluting the air.[44] They are cheap, easy for novices to use, and have insulation values up to R-40. Stuccoed on the outside, plastered inside, they make a warm, sturdy, economical, and attractive house.

How about fires, rodents, and hay fever? These hazards are more imaginary than real. Bales burn less readily than phone books (which hardly burn at all), mice can't chew through the plaster, and hay fever is a non-issue because these bales are sealed behind plaster. The one big hurdle standing in the way of greater use of straw bales is that they aren't yet approved by building codes for use in load-bearing walls. (Most new straw houses have a post-and-beam structure, with bales as in-fill.)

If you are considering any kind of new or alternative building method, be sure to explore its advantages and disadvantages in detail. Be sure, too, that it's appropriate for the local climate. Check with the local building department to see if it's code-approved.[45]

Planning—and Planting—Ahead

There's a famous story told by the late epistemologist Gregory Bateson about New College in Oxford, England. The Great Hall had been built in the early 1600s with oak beams forty feet long and two feet thick. Three hundred fifty years later, when they developed dry rot, a committee was formed to find replacement trees. They searched but couldn't find any. A young don joined the committee and said, "Why don't we ask the College Forester if some of the lands that have been given to Oxford might have suitable trees?"

When they queried the forester, he said, "We've been wondering when you would ask this question. When the Hall was constructed, the architects specified that a grove of oak trees be planted and maintained to replace the beams in the ceiling when they would suffer from dry rot. As each new forester was trained, he would be told, "Now, don't you cut any trees from that grove. Those are the trees for the Great Hall." Bateson's comment: "That's the way to run a culture."

X. ENERGY USE INSIDE

*"Our culture has adopted a design stratagem that essentially says that
if brute force or massive amounts of energy don't work,
you're not using enough of it."*
—WILLIAM MCDONOUGH, ARCHITECT, 1993

A primary goal of sustainable design is to minimize energy consumption. Once the building has been sited so that it can be daylit, heated by the sun (if desired), and built with a tight and well-insulated shell, it is time to concentrate on the energy-using equipment inside.

Over 30% of the total energy and 60% of the electricity use in the United States is in buildings. The average American family spends about $1,500 per year on household energy. Of that, space heating and appliances account for about $400 each; air conditioning and water heating, about $200 each; refrigerators, about $140; and lighting, about $100. The environmental costs—acid rain, global warming, and oil spills—don't appear on the bill, but they are real and are paid by us all.

In the commercial sector, annual costs for running a 20,000-square-foot building average about $36,000. In offices, as in homes, much energy is literally wasted by design; that is, the waste is a function of poor or sub-optimal choices made in the building's architecture, orientation, shell, insulation, glazing, and operations. Another large fraction of the waste results from a poor choice of heating and cooling systems, appliances, water heaters, lights, and office equipment.

Outfitting a green building with energy-efficient equipment has a spherical logic: it makes sense from any perspective. It saves money, reduces urban air pollution, helps protect wildlands, and improves the indoor environment.[46] For example, burning less natural gas or heating oil to warm the building will lead to corresponding reductions in smog and in CO_2, the primary greenhouse gas.

Saving electricity is even more important. Since a coal-fired power plant is only about 33% efficient to begin with, saving a unit of electricity means saving three units of fuel at the power plant. The resulting leverage can be astonishing. By installing a single compact

Efficiency for All

Energy efficiency isn't just good for the building owner; it also enriches society at large. How? The use of more efficient furnaces, motors, and appliances sharply reduces the number of new power plants needed while dramatically increasing the amount of surplus capital. For example, a $7.5 million compact-fluorescent lamp factory saves as much electricity as a $1 billion power plant makes, while avoiding the power plant's fuel cost and pollution. Net capital saving? A cool $992.5 million. (Actually more, because the power plant's capital is tied up for a decade, while the factory is quickly repaid and becomes available for prompt reinvestment.)

fluorescent lamp, for example, you can keep a power plant from emitting three-quarters of a *ton* of CO_2 and fifteen pounds of SO_2 (which causes acid rain). That one lamp also saves $30-50 worth of energy, and helps defer hundreds of dollars' worth of utility investments in new power plants. If you choose the right lamp, it will provide warm, naturally colored light with an instant start, no flicker or hum, and little glare.

When considering energy efficiency, a broad historical perspective is useful. In the past, when energy shortages loomed, the knee-jerk reaction of energy planners was to produce more: drill more oil wells, mine more coal, and build more power plants. But this "supply-side" mentality—now deeply embedded in architecture and construction—has a fatal flaw. People don't buy energy because they want to possess oily black goo, coulombs of electrons, or tons of compressed fossil swamp. What they really want are energy *services*—hot showers and cold beer, warm houses and personal mobility. Although there is growing consumer awareness and concern about environmental issues, in most cases people couldn't care less how these services are provided. But people *do* care about cost. No one wants to spend $300 a month to heat or cool their home if they can spend $30 or less for the same or better comfort and reliability.

Tackling energy problems by finding the least expensive way to provide desired energy services is called *end-use/least-cost planning*. Applying that concept to sustainable building design often yields exciting solutions.

Two years ago, Rocky Mountain Institute reviewed the basic design for a new tract home in Davis, California. Although summer temperatures there can exceed 110°F, the designers were asked to see what it would take to get rid of the cooling hardware entirely. In the process of planning a modestly air-conditioned home, they were challenged to find all applicable cooling measures—every technique, no matter how small—that might be used to reduce the cooling load further: double drywall, white roof with radiant barrier, superwindows, insulated door, and ceiling fans.

When they'd finished the first design pass, they'd come up with a house three-fifths better than Title 24 standards (the toughest in the nation) with one-and-a-quarter tons of refrigeration instead of the three-and-a-half tons they had expected. They then considered the

Cold Beer/Hot Showers

"Energy conservation" and "energy efficiency" are often used as synonyms. But there's a key difference. To many people, energy conservation implies sacrifice, "freezing in the dark," and making do with less. Energy efficiency, on the other hand, means doing more with less. It means getting the same energy services—beer just as cold, showers just as hot—while using less energy. As it turns out, energy-efficient buildings aren't just cheaper to operate; they are also nicer, more comfortable spaces in which to work and live.

other techniques and found that they added up to more than enough to make even the one-and-a-quarter tons go away. Since the air conditioner and duct work cost more than the measures that made its elimination possible, the energy-saving house cost less to build than a conventional home. And it is quieter, more comfortable, and healthier.[47] The house was completed in early 1994, and the owners love how it performs.

The same sort of systematic approach can and should be used to analyze a green building's heating, hot water, lighting, and ventilation requirements. As the Davis home illustrates, the best results come from considering *energy efficiency as a design imperative from the very start.*

Whether you build in the Northwest, where electricity costs a nickel a kilowatt-hour, or in New England, where it can be three times more expensive, it makes sense to incorporate systematically as many cost-effective efficiency improvements as possible.[48] An efficient building will typically cost about the same as a conventional one to build. A comprehensive approach to energy efficiency can even *lower* capital costs 3-5%, while reducing energy use by 50-80%.[49] For example, a ten-story office building in Pittsburgh, completed in 1983, cost $500,000 less to build and has half the operating cost of similarly sized buildings nearby.

Rocky Mountain Institute's Amory Lovins has thought a lot about the barriers to achieving energy efficiency. His thoughts on the subject:

"We've identified about 25 parties—in conception, design, finance, planning, building, maintenance, and so on ad nauseam—who all speak different languages, seldom communicate anyway, and have perfectly perverse incentives. The system penalizes efficiency and rewards inefficiency. Guess what we get!

Let me offer one example: When an architect is studying, do they ever talk to a mechanical engineer? Often, they're too busy learning how to build something that is, as they say, all glass and no windows. When they're done, they toss the drawings to the mechanical engineers, and say, "Here, cool this!" Designing a building nowadays isn't team play, it's a relay race. Fees and profits go up every time the baton is passed, and nobody's working or thinking too hard. The reason is obvious: if the building's equipment is simpler, there'll be less fee—based on cost, not on savings—and less profit.

What's needed is a way to make the rewards proportional to the performance efficiencies of the building. We think we've found one: a two-part fee, first for efficient design, then a bonus based on x% of the energy savings. The Ontario Hydro utility launched a similar program where the design team gets a rebate from the utility equal to three years' worth of energy savings. You can bet that gets their attention!"

SPACE COOLING

"In 1982, Houston residents paid $3.3 billion for cold air, more than the gross national product of 42 African nations."
—THE WALL STREET JOURNAL, 1983

In 1902, a 25-year-old engineer named Willis Haviland Carrier invented the refrigerative chiller and changed the world. Designers no longer needed to worry about form, mass, shading, orientation, or the rest of their traditional art: any sort of boxy, sealed building could be cooled by Mr. Carrier's miraculous device.

Now, ninety years later, nearly 80% of all new homes built in America are air-conditioned, compared to 58% in 1978. As a nation, we spend over $25 billion a year to stay cool, or about $100 per person. On a sweltering August afternoon, over two-fifths of utilities' power goes to cool buildings and the people inside.

The good news is that it's straightforward to design a building that can be cooled cheaply and efficiently. The key is whole-system engineering aimed at minimizing the need for mechanical cooling. This can be achieved by reducing unwanted heat gain, harnessing natural ventilation and cooling techniques, expanding occupants' "comfort envelope," and properly sizing and controlling air conditioners and other cooling equipment.

Reducing unwanted heat gain is the first step to lower cooling bills. Green office buildings and houses can stay comfortable with half to three-fourths less cooling through the use of better windows and wall and roof insulation. Building orientation, shape, mass, and roof color—topics discussed previously—play important contributory roles in reducing cooling loads, as does shading and landscaping. In hot, muggy climates, a combination of porches and shade trees around a building can dramatically reduce air temperatures inside. A final, often overlooked step in reducing cooling loads is to select efficient lights and appliances that release less waste heat inside.

Green buildings should be designed with natural ventilation in mind, not only to reduce cooling loads, but also to ensure healthy indoor air quality. The proper alignment of windows, doors, and landscaping can do much to promote air movement. Ceiling fans—which are much cheaper to operate than air conditioners—can be a valuable

A Cooling Strategy

1) Reduce cooling loads.

2) Use passive ventilation and natural cooling techniques.

3) Expand the comfort envelope with fans, dehumidifiers, seasonal attire, and better furniture design.

4) Meet the remaining load with smaller, very efficient air conditioners or evaporative coolers.

5) Optimize controls and storage (if still worthwhile).

Natural ventilation towers at the school of engineering and manufacture at DeMonfort University in Leicester, England

addition to a building's ventilation system.

In hot, dry climates, consider one of the many alternatives to mechanical cooling. For example, there is the thermal chimney, a design used in the Middle East for thousands of years. Two metal or wooden chimneys or "towers" are incorporated into the building. The downdraft tower pulls air in over a moist pad as hot air is pulled out through an updraft tower at the building's opposite end. Adding a wind scoop to the downdraft tower enables it to catch the prevailing breeze.

Depending on the climate, other passive cooling approaches, like earth sheltering, earth coupling, earth pipes, and night cooling can also be effective. Don't overlook the critical importance of thermal mass in buffering outdoor temperature swings. For example, adobe homes in Albuquerque, even uninsulated ones, will stay 15-20° F cooler than the midday peak temperature, often eliminating the need for an air conditioner. In some climates, a green office building can be cost-effectively cooled with a combined ice storage/thermal mass system.

As you design a cooling system, don't forget the human element. The perception of being hot is highly idiosyncratic. Indeed, if two people are together in the same room, one may perspire ten times more than the other. Thermal mass, natural ventilation, and passive cooling techniques will expand the comfort envelope of both. This is important since even a small expansion of the temperature range at which people feel comfortable can provide significant energy savings. Simply by increasing air movement with fans and/or lowering the humidity, people can be made much more comfortable at higher temperatures (up to 9° F).

Once everything possible has been done to reduce unwanted heat gain and expand the comfort envelope, consider how best to meet the remaining load. Different approaches to cooling are warranted in different climates. In a hot, dry climate, evaporative coolers are most effective. Indirect designs can give cool, dry air rather than adding indoor humidity. In a humid climate, a desiccant dehumidifier coupled with an efficient absorption, evaporative, or refrigerative air conditioner may be a better choice than a conventional air conditioning system.

Be forewarned that air conditioners and other cooling equipment

Roof Overhangs

In a rush to deck the roof, the carpenter snaps a line along the roof truss tails, then cuts them off. On many houses that's how roof overhang length—an absolutely critical detail for both cooling and heating—gets determined. The proper overhang (which controls window shading) is a function of climate, latitude, building orientation, and a host of other factors. It should always be calculated, not guessed.

are routinely oversized. Since an oversized cooler will cost more to buy and run, be sure yours is sized correctly. Buy the most energy-efficient model available. Its extra cost, if any, will soon be recouped in lower utility bills. Finally, be sure the conditioner is designed for the prevailing humidity levels in your climate. One that does not handle humidity well is likely to have its thermostat set lower to compensate, using more energy than necessary. With proper design, excellent dehumidification can come with dramatically higher efficiency and lower capital cost.

When buying an air conditioner, choose a model with a high Seasonal Energy Efficiency Ratio (SEER) and—to reduce peak loads—a high Energy Efficiency Ratio (EER).[50] The higher each number, the better. Ratings vary widely, are updated regularly, and are listed in the *Directory of Certified Room Air Conditioners* published by the Association of Home Appliance Manufacturers.

Once the air conditioning system is installed, be sure to operate, control, and maintain it properly.[51] Efficiency drops sharply, for example, with either too little or too much refrigerant. A set-back thermostat will save a homeowner money and energy. In an office building, use an energy management system to operate air-conditioning systems for optimal efficiency.

SPACE HEATING

"It's cheaper to save fuel than to burn it."
—AMORY LOVINS, CO-FOUNDER OF RMI, 1990

Many of the same design measures that make a green building easier to cool also make it easier to heat. The basic strategy for space heating is first to minimize heating losses through the building shell. Second, capture as much of the sun's heat as possible. Finally, meet the remaining heating load with an efficient furnace, boiler, heat pump, wood stove, or other heater. This strategy will enable you to downsize or even completely eliminate the heating system. A house that stays warm by itself—what an appealing idea!

In many climates, the best way to heat commercial and residential buildings is to combine superinsulation with passive solar design. By making the building shell as warm as possible through better insu-

Fine-tuning Performance

In the bowels of every big building is a room from which heating and cooling are controlled, often haphazardly. San Francisco engineer Zulfikar Cumali has found he can cut space-conditioning energy usage by 10% with just a half-hour of simulator training for operators. He says full control optimization, designed to fine-tune a building's performance, can save 30-50%.

lation, weatherization, and appropriate landscaping, heat losses can be reduced by half or more. The development of superwindows, with their wonderful insulating capability, makes passive solar attractive and easy to use, even in very cold climates. However, passive solar always requires careful design and suitable solar exposure. Many good books on the subject are available, including *The Passive Solar Energy Book* by Edward Mazria mentioned earlier. Note, however, that some of

Rocky Mountain Institute in midwinter

Mazria's guidelines, like those in other books written prior to the advent of superwindows, are out of date.

Residential furnaces and boilers, like air conditioners, are frequently oversized. Before sizing the system, take into account all the measures you can use to reduce the heating load. If a heating contractor or mechanical engineer does this, be sure to double-check the calculations so that you don't get stuck with an oversized model that will cost more to buy and more to operate. Standard calculations *already* include ample safety margins.

The differences in efficiency between various models of furnaces and boilers are significant. The best furnaces on the market are over 95% efficient; the average, about 75%.[53] Even if you must pay a little more up front, buying a premium-efficiency model will almost always be cost-effective.

A green office building's heating, ventilation, and air conditioning (HVAC) system should be far smaller than a conventional one. Beware of "catalog lookups" that advise you to buy a larger system than you need. Be prepared to compensate mechanical engineers or heating contractors for the extra time it may take to custom-design an efficient heating system; their extra fees, if any, will be quickly recouped in lower operating and capital costs.[55] Better still, let them

No Furnace

It's December and snowing. Sitting in Rocky Mountain Institute's 4,000-square-foot headquarters, you can watch the iguana laze in the flowering bougainvillaea, listen to the waterfall splashing into the fishponds, and wait for the bananas to ripen. Yet this superinsulated house/jungle/office, at 7,100 feet in the Rocky Mountains, has no furnace. Made of mainly local materials in 1982-84, it is heated by the sun, with two wood stoves for backup, photovoltaics, and solar hot water. It saves 90% of the household electricity, 99% of the space and water heating energy, and half the water of a normal house. The $1.50/square foot marginal cost of its energy savings paid back in ten months with 1983 technology.[52]

keep part of the life-cycle cost they save you, so they have an incentive to do the calculations for real optimization.

Furnaces and boilers can operate on a variety of fuels, including natural gas, heating oil, propane, and coal. Of the fossil fuels, natural gas is the cheapest and cleanest to use when it's available. Radiant floor heating, although somewhat costly to install, is an extremely comfortable heat source and, since there are no fumes or dust, is especially good for people with allergies or chemical sensitivities.

How about wood heat? There are arguments for and against it. Although properly harvested wood is a renewable resource, older wood stoves emit 200-1,000 times the particulates of a gas furnace; newer stoves are ten times cleaner than the old ones, but still relatively dirty.[56] Fireplaces, wood stoves, and pellet stoves can also contribute to indoor air quality problems. Wood stoves *sometimes* make sense as backup heat in a sustainable home, but fireplaces almost *never* do, because most of their heat goes up the chimney. If you want a fireplace for aesthetics, be sure to provide it with outside combustion air and a tight-fitting damper. When buying a wood stove, make sure that it meets Environmental Protection Agency regulations and is correctly sized for the space it will heat.

Although it costs two to three times as much to heat a building with electricity than with gas, there are certain situations where electric heat may make sense—if the climate is very mild and heat is rarely needed, or if the occupants suffer from chemical sensitivity and cannot use gas for health reasons.[57] However, if you do heat with electricity, be sure to build a weathertight, well-insulated building. It's also wise to choose an electric heat pump rather than electric baseboards. Although air-source heat pumps are not appropriate for all climates (those places where the air temperature routinely drops below freezing), they are typically much cheaper to operate than baseboards. Water or ground-source heat pumps can better tolerate low outdoor temperature. But superinsulation is usually an even better buy.

As buildings become tighter and air quality concerns grow, air-to-air heat exchangers gain new importance. An exchanger can recover 80% of the temperature differential between incoming and exhaust air while preserving air quality. These systems, which can be installed for individual rooms or for an entire building, are far more energy-efficient and healthier than opening windows during cold, hot, or polluted times of the year.

Bigelow's Guarantee

Chicago-area builder Perry Bigelow guarantees that his homes' heating bills won't exceed $200—annually. If they do, he pays the difference. Bigelow builds about 100 homes a year, but hasn't had to pay out a dime since the late 1980s. How does he do it? With R-25 walls, R-38 ceilings, low-e argon-filled windows (but not yet true superwindows), and meticulous weatherization. In many Bigelow homes, the gas water heater acts as the only furnace. All the efficiency measures together add only $600 to the house's price.[54]

Any heating system should be properly controlled.[58] For example, a programmable thermostat can save roughly 6-16% of heating energy by automatically turning down the furnace at night and raising it again in the morning.[59] Most commercial buildings should use a computerized energy management system (EMS) to operate their heating and cooling systems. An EMS manages temperatures, turning furnaces and air conditioners on and off as needed. It can also control lights. Looking ahead, the "distributed intelligence" systems that are now being developed will enable building operators to control appliances, lights, and heating and cooling systems at their points of use. These systems may revolutionize office building control technology when they become widely available. Installing an EMS before other efficiency measures will mask your ability to realize larger energy savings and is not, by itself, an optimal solution.[60]

ELECTRIC LIGHTING

"Efficient lighting is not just a free lunch;
it's a lunch you are paid to eat."
—AMORY LOVINS, CO-FOUNDER OF RMI, 1987

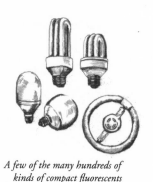

A few of the many hundreds of kinds of compact fluorescents

Lighting buildings accounts for about 20% of U.S. electricity consumption. But recent developments in energy-efficient lighting make it possible to save about three-fourths of that energy cost-effectively. These new options include fluorescent lamp tubes the thickness of a pencil, solid-state electronic ballasts, imaging specular reflectors, pocket-sized compact fluorescent lamps, "smart" light bulbs with built-in controls, and an array of new lighting fixtures. The lighting revolution is being driven by technological advances, economic and environmental concerns (the Environmental Protection Agency's Green Lights Program has had a big impact), and utility energy-efficiency programs.

When designing lighting for a building, take a systems approach. Remember that worker productivity, lighting quality, energy efficiency, security, safety, maintenance, and economics are all interrelated. Don't forget that people should come first. Since different people perceive light quality, quantity, and color differently, have different visual abilities, and even have different "appetites" for light at different times of the day or year, a lighting system must be flexible and adjustable.

Design lighting according to the specific needs of a given space. First, use glare-free, well-distributed daylighting to minimize the need for electric light. Second, use high-quality, efficient, and properly controlled electric lighting. Third, be sure to consider the different illumination levels and color contrasts required in different rooms, buildings, and building types. Fourth, it's typically about ten times as important to reduce "veiling glare"—stray light that washes out contrast—as to add more light. That's why you can see at least as well with 20 glare-free indirect footcandles bounced off the ceiling as with 100 "glary" direct footcandles from downlighting.

In general, a good design will offer ambient lighting for background and space definition, task lighting for individual detail work, and accent lighting to add "sparkle" to a space.[61] Provide light only where, when, and in the amount needed: don't light an entire room brightly if the only place you need it is at a desk. Place adjustable task lights in areas where reading, writing, cooking, or other meticulous work is performed.[62]

In new commercial construction, the payback for an efficient lighting system strategy is immediate, because the capital costs saved by downsizing the cooling system typically exceed the extra costs of providing better lighting. Residences can also achieve significant savings from efficient lighting. In addition, utilities in many areas offer hefty rebates for efficient lighting—incentives that make it even more attractive to install.

Compact fluorescent lamps should be used instead of incandescent lamps for virtually all ambient lighting in residential buildings. CFLs produce pleasant, "warm-colored" light, use a quarter as much electricity as incandescents, and last about ten times as long. They can be used in most conventional lighting fixtures and are available in many different sizes, shapes, and wattages.[63] When you buy CFLs, consider those that plug into a separate electronic ballast. The two-piece fixtures may be slightly more expensive initially than one-piece CFLs. However, since the ballasts last four to seven times as long as the lamps, the modular units are cheaper over the long run and are also available in dimmable models. Two-piece compact fluorescents are available from most major lighting manufacturers.[64]

Compact Fluorescents

Standard incandescent lights are really tiny space heaters that just happen to give off a little light: over 90% of the energy they use ends up as heat. Often, this heat has to be removed by a air conditioner, wasting yet more money. Replacing incandescent lamps with efficient compact fluorescent lamps (CFLs) lowers utility bills and reduces cooling loads. CFLs last five to thirteen times longer than incandescents and save $30 to $50 in energy bills over their lifetime.

Tubular fluorescent lamps are used for ambient lighting in many commercial buildings. However, note that all fluorescent tubes are not equally efficient. Old-style T-12s use significantly more energy than the newer T-8s, and their color isn't as pleasant, accurate, or easy to see with. Be sure to specify electronic ballasts, not core-coil ones. The latter have a noticeable flicker and hum and are less efficient. If you can, triple the savings from the ballasts and controls by getting continuous dimming electronic ballasts, not fixed-output models.

To save even more lighting energy, use motion sensors. When someone enters an area, the lights automatically turn on. When no motion is detected after a specified period, the lights shut off. Motion sensors are particularly useful in offices, basements, bathrooms, and other rooms where people tend to forget to turn off the lights. With dimming ballasts, you can also use controls that automatically dim or brighten the lamps to compensate for daylighting, age, or dirt.

A final reminder: as wonderful as many of the new lighting products are, they can be, and often are, misused. The new products must be used *in appropriate fixtures and applications.* Since one size does not fit all, "don't force the fit." CFLs may require harp extenders or other modifications to fit into older fixtures. Many new fixtures are designed specifically for CFLs. Efficiency and lifetime can drop if CFLs get overheated or mounted in the wrong positions. Energy-efficient lighting is as much about the proper *application* of technology as it is about the technology itself.

WATER HEATERS

"A 'cheap' $425 electric tank heater can cost you $5,902 (fourteen times its purchase price) in energy costs over its typical thirteen-year life."
—RMI HOME ENERGY BRIEF, 1994

After space heating and cooling, the largest energy user in the typical home is the water heater. Americans collectively spend $15 billion a year to heat water; the average family spends $190 a year to heat water with gas or $430 with electricity.

A natural-gas-fired water heater costs less than half as much to operate as does an electric one, so where gas is available, it's the preferred choice. When using an electric heater, make sure it's insulated to R-16 or better. (Some newer models come this well insulated; older ones can be cheaply and easily retrofitted with an insulating blanket.)

Any type of water heater will be much cheaper to operate if it supports a reduced load: the installation of water-efficient showerheads and faucet aerators should be standard practice in green buildings. Using energy-management practices in conjunction with water-efficient hardware will increase your savings. For example, reducing the thermostat on water heaters to 120°F—or even less using enzymatic dishwashing detergents—and using an automatic timer to turn the heater off at night are cost-effective ways to save even more energy. Proper insulation and layout of pipes is also important.

Rather than using a conventional tank-type hot-water heater, consider using an alternative system for water heating. On-demand water heaters, solar water heaters, and desuperheaters all have attractive advantages. On-demand heaters differ from conventional ones in that they do not have a storage tank. Buildings that have moderate or easily scheduled hot water requirements will find on-demand heaters much more efficient than a standard water heater.[65] They are very common in Europe and readily available in the U.S.

Solar water heating has come a long way since the 1970s, and there are now a number of very attractive, reliable and frostproof models on the market. Some are completely passive rooftop models. In many parts of the U.S., there is no reason why a house or office building should not use the sun to heat its water. Although solar water heaters do have longer payback periods than "traditional" water heaters; they can save lots of energy and pollution.

Solar water heaters can heat water for domestic, commercial, or industrial uses, including hydronic space heating (radiant floors). In the U.S., collectors should be mounted facing south for maximum solar exposure.[66] The correct tilt angle is a function of latitude. Proper installation and maintenance are essential. Although the federal tax credit for solar hot water systems has long since expired, many states still offer tax credits for their use in industrial and, sometimes, domestic applications.[67]

Two other water heating alternatives to consider are desuperheaters and, for larger buildings, cogeneration. A desuperheater preheats water for commercial and residential applications by transferring waste heat from the condensers of air conditioners or refrigeration systems.[68] It works best in warm climates, or in cooling constantly overheated spaces like restaurant kitchens.

Cogeneration is the production of electricity, heat, and/or hot water from a single power source. It can be very cost-effective for small manufacturers, laundromats, health clubs, hospitals, car washes, some restaurants, and other commercial buildings that use a lot of electricity and hot water. For example, Kaiser Hospital spent $90,000 to install seven cogeneration units in three hospitals. They save $28,000 to $30,000 annually. Cogeneration saves Paradise Hill Convalescent Home in San Diego $3,500 per month. As a rule, cogeneration is most cost-effective for businesses whose water and electricity bills exceed $1,000 a month. The typical payback period is about three years.

APPLIANCES

"Our climate change program helps companies and consumers save energy and money with air conditioners, computers, refrigerators and lightbulbs that use less electricity than ever before."
—PRESIDENT CLINTON, EARTH DAY SPEECH, 1994

Ideally, all the appliances in a green home should be as efficient as possible. At the very least, homes should have an efficient refrigerator, clothes washer, and clothes dryer—the three appliances that use the most energy. Small differences, if any, in the cost of efficient appliances will be rapidly repaid in energy savings.[69] Similar opportunities, often at no extra cost, exist for virtually all other kinds of appliances, from dishwashers to televisions.

To find efficient models, start by comparing the "Energy Guide" labels found on many appliances. *The Consumer Guide to Home Energy Savings*, updated annually and found in most large bookstores, can help in the selection process. The environmental impact of manufacturing and disposing of appliances is high, so choose sturdy, well-built ones that will have long lives.

Refrigerators have grown more efficient in recent years, but they still use lots of energy. The good news is that in 1994, Whirlpool introduced a refrigerator that is 30% more efficient than 1993 models. Other manufacturers will no doubt follow suit. This new refrigerator does not use ozone-damaging chlorofluorocarbons (CFCs) as a refrigerant or as a blowing agent for their foam insulation.[70] It should retail at prices comparable to conventional models. Still further improvements are in store.

Top-loading washing machines use a great deal of water and energy. Instead, consider buying a horizontal-axis machine. Widely used in Europe but almost unheard of in America, these machines use 60% less energy and 40% less water and detergent than the most efficient vertical-axis machines.[71] Check *The Consumer Guide to Home Energy Savings* or Rocky Mountain Institute's *The Energy Efficient Home* for more information. Since approximately 90% of the energy used by a washing machine is for heating water, use warm/cold-water wash cycles and cold rinse cycles instead of hot.

When buying a new clothes dryer, consider one that has a moisture sensor rather than a timer. Moisture sensors prevent excessive drying and save up to 15% of the energy used. Don't put the dryer in a basement or unheated space. Of course, a clothes line is the most energy-efficient and environmentally friendly way to dry clothes.

OFFICE EQUIPMENT

"The EPA estimates that the Energy Star program should save up to $1 billion worth of electricity each year—enough to power all of Vermont and New Hampshire."
—RMI HOME ENERGY BRIEF, 1994

Computers. Copiers. Printers. Fax machines. It is hard to imagine a world without electronic office equipment. Yet until recently, office equipment users have been largely oblivious to economic, energy, and environmental costs. This is now changing, as energy rating systems combine with technological advances to signal a new era for energy-saving office products.

The proliferation in the numbers of office equipment has been extremely rapid. Eight years ago, office equipment wasn't even recognized as a distinct end-use of electricity. Today, it accounts for the consumption of 30 billion kilowatt-hours each year—a staggering 5% of the electricity in the commercial sector. This could grow to 10%

by the year 2000. This load has a number of profound implications for green office buildings. Intensive electricity use by office equipment increases peak power demand, utility bills, and pollution. More importantly, it increases cooling loads. In many new buildings, there is a direct link between the efficiency of office equipment and the capital costs for the cooling system. Since efficient office equipment produces less waste heat, a decrease of just 1 watt per square foot in the average plug load can decrease the capital cost for the cooling system of a large commercial building by approximately $1 per square foot.

The good news is that recent technological developments enable office equipment to be made much more energy-efficient. Encouraging this trend is the goal of the EPA's Energy Star program. To date, companies representing about 70% of the computer market and 90% of the laser printer market have signed on. Many manufacturers are already building machines that meet Energy Star criteria without sacrificing performance or increasing price. Similar efficiency targets exist or are being developed for monitors, printers, and other office equipment. All these standards are likely to continue to improve.

Laptop or notebook computers are very energy-efficient and allow you to work anywhere. Older models of laser printers use lots of energy. Using an ink-jet or bubble-jet printer instead will save energy and money. If a laser printer is a necessity, buy an Energy Star one. Other kinds of printers can also be big energy users, so shop carefully.

Photocopiers are often real energy hogs. Their overall efficiency is typically a function of power consumption and copy speed. Most manufacturers do have models that are reasonably efficient, so it is worthwhile to ask about the options.[72] You can save energy both by shopping carefully for the right model (ask for its ASTM energy ratings) and by using its "energy saving" button.

Indonesian Wisdom

Dutch scientist Dr. Kees Daey Ouwens helped an Indonesian village, which had a power line running right past it, save money by not hooking up. He equipped each house with solar cells and efficient lights, radios, and other appliances. The villagers will pay for these over ten years. But they have a positive cashflow from the beginning—because servicing the debt costs less than they were paying for lamp kerosene and radio batteries. If Third World villagers can finance solar electricity and save money on the deal, why can't industrial nations?

RENEWABLE ENERGY

"A building should be like a tree, it should thrive on the sun's energy, while enhancing its surroundings."
—WILLIAM MCDONOUGH, ARCHITECT, 1993

Most existing green buildings are connected to the grid and get their electricity from coal-, nuclear-, or natural-gas-powered plants. With the possible exception of buildings in the Northwest and other regions where hydroelectric dams supply the bulk of the power, this is not, in the long run, sustainable. Ideally, a green building would get not just its daylight and heat, but also its *electricity* from the sun or other renewable energy sources.

Although electricity from photovoltaics (PVs), windpower, and other renewables often remains somewhat more expensive than that from power plants, the number of situations in which renewables are the most economic form of energy continues to grow.[73] Two trends are converging to make renewables more attractive than ever. First, as appliances, lights, and office equipment become more energy-efficient, it becomes easier and cheaper to meet a house's electricity needs. Second, the past decade has seen dramatic improvements in PVs, windpower, and micro-hydro technology. Costs are falling and reliability is increasing. There have also been tremendous improvements in controllers and AC inverters—the brains of most alternative energy systems. As buildings become increasingly energy-efficient and technological improvements continue, renewable energy becomes more practical and less costly each year. In windy areas, windpower has been the cheapest source of new power for many years.

While it's still not economically feasible for most urban buildings to go "off the grid," using renewables to meet some or all of a building's energy needs often *does* make sense, particularly in rural areas where it may cost $10,000 or more to extend a power line one mile. If the building site is more than a quarter-mile from a power line, efficiently used PVs are likely to be a cheaper source of power than connecting to the grid.

In many states, public utilities are now required to inform you if it is cheaper to install PVs than hook up to the utility grid.[74] Some

Homeowner Hydro

Norm Benzinger, owner of Coulter Lake Guest Ranch, a wilderness retreat in the Rockies, had a problem. The ranch's propane bill had topped $10,000 in 1992—one-quarter of it consumed by a generator. Hoping to slash his energy costs, Norm installed a micro-hydroelectric turbine on a nearby stream. Now the generator, which used to drone for hours a day, has fallen silent. A water power system that cost $6,000 will save $2,500 in its first winter.

utilities even lease or subsidize PV systems to relieve building owners of the large capital cost of purchasing an alternative system. The utility often saves money on the deal because it does not have to pay for the line or capacity extension.

The economics of renewable energy can be even better if you've got a good windpower or, rarer still, hydro or geothermal site. Commercial wind turbines now generate power for about 5 cents a kilowatt-hour in good sites; micro-hydro and geothermal can be cheaper still.

Harvesting windpower

But PVs and other renewables aren't just for rural areas. For example, the Sacramento Municipal Utility District and other far-sighted utilities are beginning to install rooftop PV systems to support their grid, help meet peak power demands, and reduce dependence on traditional sources of power. Southern California Edison has announced plans for a similar program, and other utilities are studying the idea. Although the number of PV-powered buildings is still small, interest in integrating PVs into building projects is growing worldwide. In Japan, for example, the government has announced plans to subsidize 70,000 rooftop systems by the year 2000. A number of European countries are undertaking similar programs.

PV prices are likely to fall some more, so it makes sense for green building designers to plan for that eventuality. The key thing to remember is that efficiency and renewables go hand in hand. If you have hopes of using renewables now or later, be sure to minimize the building's energy requirements—and design for easy addition of PVs in the not-too-distant future.

XI. Saving Water

"When the well's dry, we know the worth of water."
—Benjamin Franklin, Statesman and Scientist, ~ 1790

Water is a precious resource that should be used efficiently indoors and out. Saving water saves money—but the ramifications of water efficiency go far beyond lower utility bills.

The supply of clean, unpolluted water is finite, as is wastewater treatment capacity. Installing water-efficient plumbing fixtures in a green building will reduce the load at sewage treatment plants while helping to protect free-flowing rivers and the trout, ducks, and other wildlife dependent on them. Tucson, Memphis, and hundreds of other cities pump their drinking water from underground; in these places, water efficiency can help extend the lifetime of aquifers.

Water ought to be saved for these reasons, but also because it contains a large quantity of embodied energy. As water travels from river to house to sewage plant, energy is used to pump it, treat it, heat it, pump it back, and treat it again. Whenever water can be saved, so can energy, and the energy savings often financially dwarf the water savings.

Saving water is easy and inexpensive. The installation in new buildings of low-flush toilets, efficient showerheads, faucet aerators, and efficient appliances (such as horizontal-axis washing machines) can cut water use by 30% or more. These efficient devices provide the same or better service, at comparable prices. Retrofits are also easy. Installing efficient showerheads and faucet aerators will cut the average household's water and energy bills by $59 to $119 each year. Not bad for an hour's work.

When saving water, avoid gadgets and gimmicks. Low-flow toilets that use 1.5 gallons per flush work a lot better than a 5-gallon model with a brick or a dam in the tank. All toilets are designed to flush with a specific amount of water. Yet high-performance toilets discharge their reduced water volume in a narrow pulse that has several times the flow velocity of 5- or 3.5-gallon models, and so provide better transport.

A blizzard of water-efficient faucets, toilets, showerheads, and other plumbing fixtures has come on the market in recent years. For

Two Success Stories

In 1985, Pennsylvania's Edinboro University retrofitted its dorms with water-efficient fixtures at a one-time cost of $11,000. Annual savings in water, sewer, and energy bills have since averaged $52,000. In Maryland, the state Water Conservation Office retrofitted a senior citizens' center with 1.6-gallon toilets to free up sewer capacity so that it could get permission to build fifty new apartments. The program cost $16,000. That is $119,000 less than it would otherwise have cost to secure water and sewer rights for the apartments.

example, there are at least thirty different models of efficient showerheads with spray styles that range from misty to blasting to pulsating.[75] The new hardware not only meets all building codes; in many places it is now required.

In January 1994, new national standards for plumbing fixtures went into effect. The following chart summarizes the new delivery rate criteria.

Appliance	Delivery rate in gallons per minute
Kitchen faucets	2.5 or less
Bathroom faucets	2.5 or less
Showerheads	2.5 or less
Toilets and flush valves	1.6 or less per flush
Urinals and flush valves	1.0 or less per flush

Note that many fixtures beat these standards, and that manufacturers and stores are allowed to sell older, less efficient plumbing hardware until their stock runs out.

WATER-EFFICIENT LANDSCAPING

Because water touches on so many other economic and environmental issues, its efficient use should be a primary concern in the development of a landscaping plan for a green building or development. The proper selection of plants, irrigation equipment, and irrigation scheduling can dramatically reduce water waste. Although outdoor water use varies widely from place to place and climate to climate, an average of about 50% of residential water use occurs outside. Much of this water is wasted—either because it's applied to inappropriate landscaping (Kentucky bluegrass in Las Vegas), or because it's applied in the wrong way at the wrong time in the wrong quantities. It's a common summertime sight to see sprinklers on at noon on a hot sunny day, half the water evaporating before it even hits the ground, and much of the rest running down the streets.

For example, the Cathedral City Country Club in Riverside, California reduced water use 70% and saved $32,000 per year in pumping costs by improving irrigation technologies and management practices. A survey of 1,000 homes in Oakland, California found that those with water-efficient landscapes used 42% less water or 209 fewer gallons a day.

Although parts of the eastern U.S. receive sufficient rainfall to grow just about anything, in the arid west the story is different. There, landscaping with native, drought-tolerant species rather than thirsty exotics like bluegrass will save both water and maintenance costs. In the desert areas of the west, the use of water-frugal techniques known as "xeriscaping" can dramatically slash outdoor water consumption.

Similarly, installing a drip irrigation system to water trees, bushes, and shrubs will reduce water use. If an automatic sprinkler system is installed, be sure it's programmed correctly to maximize the benefits of irrigation. It's best to water deeply every four days, rather than shallowly every two.[77] This reduces total water consumption and is better for the plants. The best irrigation timers also include buried moisture sensors that enable you to deliver just the right amount of water to the root zone; rather than having to water because you're not sure.

Perhaps the best way to save large quantities of water, labor, and money is to downsize or even eliminate the area dedicated to turf. Again, the question is one of scale. A small lawn is nice for the kids to play on. But do you really want to play barber to 5,000 or 10,000 square feet of grass? Many lawns end up being so big simply because the building site is completely denuded during site preparation. Installing a lawn then becomes a cheap (at least initially) way to camouflage the devastation. Instead, try to preserve existing trees and treat the yard as a series of rooms with different uses.

RAINWATER COLLECTION

From an environmental perspective, the practice of using treated water to irrigate lawns and bushes is a bit absurd. One way for a green building to reduce its need for treated water is to capture rainwater onsite, in either a cistern or a manmade catchment basin. This will reduce the amount of potable water a building consumes while enlarging its supply of landscaping water. Both cisterns and catchment basins are ancient ways of meeting some or all of a building's water needs. On the island of Hawaii, 25,000 people rely on rainwater for their entire water supply, including landscaping and potable uses.

Cisterns are usually fed with water from the roof. A simple system of gutters captures run-off and channels it to an above- or below-ground cistern. Catchment areas, which are often landscaped to look

Landscape Rebates

Mesa, Arizona refunds up to 25% of its water tap fee to homeowners or developers who install water-efficient landscaping. As of October 1992, 2,394 participants had received over $1 million. On average, their homes use about 40% less water than their neighbors' with turf-intensive landscapes.

An example of a cistern

like ponds or marshes, can also be fed with water taken from roofs or with water draining from paved and turf areas. Surface swales can be used to channel the run-off to where it will be stored. Capturing and reusing rainwater works as well in cities as it does in the country. In downtown Tokyo, for example, a wrestling arena has its own 250,000-gallon cistern.

Costs for installing a rainwater collection system depend on its size. Systems that will meet all household needs are often comparable to the cost of drilling a well. Some cities may not allow you to disconnect from the municipal water system, but you can just use it as a back-up.

WASTEWATER

The average American household generates over 75,000 gallons of wastewater each year. But the term "wastewater" bears rethinking. The vast majority of this water is from sinks, showers, baths, dishwashers, and clothes washers—not toilets—and could safely be put to other uses.

Here, the analogy of "cascading uses" is helpful. Ideally, treated water should *only* be used for cooking, drinking, bathing, and cleaning clothes and dishes. Water from showers, sinks, and washing machines—usually called graywater—can be used to flush toilets or for landscaping. Sewage or "blackwater" from toilets must be treated, but then the resulting effluent can also be used to water golf courses or other landscaping.

Historically, most plumbing codes have flatly forbidden the use of graywater. But now many communities are taking a second look. Although some jurisdictions still prohibit graywater use, others have begun to permit it, including the entire state of California. In most cases, you must install separate drain lines and where applicable, separate septic tanks, to keep graywater and blackwater separate. This is not overly difficult or expensive in new construction. Retrofits are another issue; the costs may outweigh the benefits, particularly for small buildings that are already using water efficiently.

The typical U.S. household will produce about 50 gallons of graywater per person per day. In many cases, the availability of this water can make the difference between minimal and lush landscaping. Before being used for irrigation, graywater should be passed through a commercial filter or a site-built sand filter. After filtration, it is safe to use graywater on most plantings.

ALTERNATIVE SEWAGE SYSTEMS

There are a number of alternatives to conventional sewage systems. And while they don't save water *per se*, they do have many other environmental and economic benefits. So-called biological wastewater systems are designed to mimic nature. Some of these biological systems are set up as an interlinked series of wetlands and marshes. Others treat the waste in a large greenhouse or use algal turf scrubber systems.

How do they work? In a marsh-type system, sewage water passes through a series of wetlands where it is purified by water-loving plants and microorganisms, eventually emerging cleaner than Class 1 drinking water. The approach is low-cost, low-maintenance, and low-tech, but it does require a fair amount of land. That obstacle is overcome with the greenhouse or "solar aquatics" approach, where wastewater passes through a series of tanks and is gradually purified by plants, bacteria, invertebrates, fish, and sunlight.

These systems share certain advantages. First, they use much less energy and capital, and far fewer chemicals, than do conventional sewage plants.[78] Second, they are cheaper to operate. Third, they are surprisingly attractive. In at least one place, they are being used as the educational centerpiece of a school. Fourth, they provide natural habitat, fertilizer, and in some cases food. Frederick, Maryland, is installing a biological waste treatment system to treat the wastewater from thousands of buildings. Experts will compare the water output from this system to conventional (tertiary) wastewater treatment. The city expects that the biological system will do a better job of eliminating nitrogen and phosphorus from the water, thereby reducing algae blooms in Chesapeake Bay.

Although single buildings are generally too small to sustain a biological wastewater system, a cluster of buildings or a subdivision

Graywater Flushes

The Apple Farm Inn in San Luis Obispo, California is a luxury hotel adjacent to a 250-seat restaurant. Graywater from the hotel's clothes washers is used to flush the toilets in the restaurant restrooms. Annual water savings are about $5,000. The system has worked so well that the owners are exploring the possibility of using graywater from the laundry to flush toilets in the Inn's rooms as well.

could. The cost-effectiveness of biological wastewater treatment depends on the site location, size, and other factors.[79]

An alternative sewage option for individual homes is a composting toilet. These work well in situations where installing a septic system is forbidden, expensive, or impossible—where, for example, the building site is adjacent to a river, or the ground is underlain by solid rock or permafrost. Composting toilets have the great advantage of not requiring water to operate. The end product can be used as a fertilizer. Since they are biological systems, they require regular maintenance. They also have many disadvantages—they can smell, they can't adapt to irregular or pulse usage, they must be regularly maintained—and may make it difficult to resell the house.

Solar aquatic wastewater treatment system

XII. Building Ecology

*"I durst not laugh, for fear of opening my lips
and receiving the bad air."*
—Shakespeare, Julius Caesar, 1599

The term "building ecology" refers to the physical environment, particularly the air quality, found inside a structure. A building's ecology can be good or bad. It is affected by a number of factors, including the kind of materials and finishes used in the building's construction, the quality of heating, cooling, and ventilation systems, and operation and maintenance practices. Although air quality is the key issue in building ecology, acoustics and electromagnetic fields are related concerns.

INDOOR AIR QUALITY

As buildings become tighter and are filled with manufactured building materials, an unexpected danger can crop up—poor indoor air quality.

Believe it or not, the air quality inside many urban buildings can be much worse than the acrid smog outside. The phenomenon of "sick building" syndrome is caused, in part, by the "outgassing" of chemical compounds from paints, carpets, particle board, and construction adhesives.[80] But outgassing isn't the only cause of poor air quality. Inadequately vented appliances, cigarette smoke, radon, noxious vapors from cleaning compounds, airborne bacteria and molds, human and pet dandruff, microscopic dust mites, and even the use of vacuum cleaners can contribute to sick buildings.

One of the first steps in protecting or improving air quality is to ensure that the air coming into the building is clean. Locate incoming air ducts away from driveways and loading docks, exhaust air ducts, and garbage dumpsters. If needed, install a filtration system to remove contaminants and pollutants.

Adequate ventilation in buildings is crucial, since most people spend 80% of their time indoors. Historically, this has meant providing a specified number of "air changes" per hour.[81] Such standards, however, may not ensure adequate air mixing or may induce unnecessarily high ventilation rates. A new, more promising strategy is to use air monitoring sensors. For example, CO_2 sensors can be used in commercial buildings. CO_2 levels go up when air quality decreases, so by increasing or decreasing ventilation rates as needed, the sensors prevent stuffiness without wasting energy by ventilating more than is needed.

In a commercial building with a combined heating, cooling, and ventilation system, make sure proper air mixing occurs. Air-handling ducts should also be sealed to prevent the breeding of molds and mildew. Ducts should be cleaned after installation and on a regular basis thereafter by competent, licensed cleaners.

Heat recovery ventilation systems (HRVs), more commonly known as air-to-air heat exchangers, are being used in growing numbers of homes to preserve indoor air quality. They can exhaust particulates and volatile organic compounds (VOCs) while recovering 80% of the temperature difference between incoming and exhaust air. HRVs are much better than windows for ventilating a house when the weather is bad or outside air conditions are poor.

A sustainable building's ventilation and filtration systems should be carefully designed to filter out pollutants and toxins. After installing any ventilation system, check to make sure it is working properly. On large buildings, it's a good idea to hire an independent consultant to "commission" the mechanical systems.

The choice of materials used to construct, finish, and furnish a building is also important. Of the hundreds of different materials, paints, and finishes used in construction, most are non-toxic. But that leaves dozens that, to one degree or another, *are* toxic. Products containing lead and asbestos have been outlawed. But it may also be wise to avoid those products that outgas formaldehyde, many organic solvents, and chlorofluorocarbons. Finally, avoid products that tend to propagate bacteria, dust mites, and molds.

As a rule, a healthy building should strive for at least a 50% reduction of normal levels of known contaminants (it is possible to exceed 90% if necessary to protect someone who is chemically sensitive). To achieve either standard, one must be particular about choosing paints and finishes. Oil-based paints and solvent-based finishes like polyurethane give off fumes that can cause nausea, tremors, headaches, and, some doctors believe, longer-lasting harm. The symptoms are caused by VOCs, a class of chemical compounds.

Use low—or ideally no—VOC finishes. These water-based products often require fewer coats per surface, are quite durable, and are increasingly price-competitive with conventional finishes. There is no disposal problem or risk of ground water contamination from many of these finishes. When the health and productivity of the building's occupants, or even disposal costs, are factored in, the additional expense, if any, of no-VOC coatings is easily justified.

Many green building products have been formulated especially to reduce outgassing. For example, reformulated joint compounds eliminate over 90% of the toxic and carcinogenic components of conventional joint compound. Be sure to choose these materials, specify that they be used, and carefully monitor any substitutions made during the construction process.

In new construction, store building materials outside for a couple of weeks—protected from the weather—before using them. This will allow VOCs to escape outside, rather than inside. As the building nears completion, open the windows and run the ventilation systems to "flush out" the remaining VOCs. A "bake out"—heating the building to a high temperature for an extended period—is *not* recommended. It was once believed that this would cause outgassing to occur more rapidly. However, the process can damage building materials and cause other surfaces to absorb the outgassed toxins.

Cigarette smoking should not be allowed in new buildings. If smoking is allowed, restrict it to outside areas away from entries and windows or to specific rooms that are vented to the outside.

Rooms that contain pools, hot tubs, or spas often have decreased air quality because of the chemicals used to treat the water. Photocopier rooms and darkrooms are other places where air quality is typically poor. Such rooms should be ventilated directly to the outside to prevent the buildup of noxious fumes. Vent-type hookups for photocopiers, not unlike dryer vents, do exist; however, regularly scheduled replacement of their ozone-absorbing canisters, plus an air-to-air heat exchanger, make a better choice for maintaining air quality.

Finally, watch out for mold and mildew in kitchens, bathrooms, and other high-humidity areas. Consider installing heat-recovery ventilators to ensure adequate ventilation to inhibit mold growth. Daylighting will also help.

Cleanliness may be next to godliness, but it must be done with care. Many commercial cleaning products are highly toxic. Most vacuum cleaners are ineffective at filtering out dust particles and can actually worsen indoor air quality. Suspended particles blown from vacuum exhaust can linger in the air for an hour or more. The best vacuums have high-efficiency filters (sometimes called HEPA filters) and strong suction capability.

ACOUSTICS

The need for pleasant acoustics is often overlooked in building design. Acoustics are important because of their powerful effect on human productivity, attention span, and stress level. A loud, noisy, jarring building is a disagreeable place. On the other hand, soothing acoustics will add immeasurably to occupants' comfort.

An energy-efficient building is usually quieter than a conventional one due to its smaller heating, ventilation, and air conditioning (HVAC) system, better designed air distribution fans, and noise-blocking superwindows. On the other hand, hard-surfaced, thermal mass areas may cause echoes and reverberations. Opening windows for natural ventilation may also allow unwanted noises into the building. However, it is possible to mitigate these effects. For example, landscaping and earthen berms (which may already be in use to help reduce HVAC loads) can dampen road sounds, while an indoor fountain or water sculpture can mask unwanted indoor noises.

ELECTROMAGNETIC FIELDS

There is some evidence to suggest that electromagnetic fields (EMF) may be linked to cancer, miscarriages, and other disorders. These fields occur whenever alternating current runs through an operating appliance or wire. These invisible waves weaken over distance, so that exposure to a nearby electric razor or hair dryer may be more harmful than exposure to distant power lines. More definitive research is needed to determine the real danger caused by EMF.

However, in the meantime, a practice of "prudent avoidance" is being widely adopted by green builders.

In general, an energy-efficient building will have lower EMF levels than a conventional one. However, take care to reduce exposure to power lines, electrical wiring, household appliances, and office equipment. Select sites at least 100 yards away from power lines or transformers. During construction, try to reduce EMF by placing distribution transformers back-to-back (so their magnetic fields cancel) and ensuring that wiring is properly installed. When wiring a building, it may be worth the modest extra expense to install "twisted-pair" wiring so that the electrical fields cancel each other out. It's possible to purchase appliances and equipment that have low EMF levels. It's also possible to make a few simple changes in lifestyle. Staying three to five feet away from appliances, two feet from computer screens, and three to ten feet from microwave ovens when they are operating will reduce exposure.

Research about EMF is ongoing. Local utilities may have more information and, perhaps, a gaussmeter that can be borrowed to measure EMF levels in the building or on the site.

Power lines

No VOCs Please

The architect for the Body Shop headquarters wanted to use no-VOC paints but she ran into a problem. The paints cost $2 more per gallon, and there was no room in the budget. She asked the manufacturer if they could do anything to help. They promptly cut their bid by the marginal cost of the paints. The painting contractor was thrilled. No-VOC paints require no primer, go on more smoothly, and the painters don't have to go outside to breathe periodically. That doesn't even count the reduction in compliance costs for OSHA standards. These factors can lower labor costs by more than one third. Disposal costs also drop dramatically. Regular paints (and cans) must be disposed of in special fifty-gallon drums (at $200 each). So in this one case, using no-VOC paints was good for the American manufacturer who got one more demonstration of its product's quality; the Body Shop's employees who enjoy better indoor air quality; the architect who got to use the more environmentally sound product; the painting contractor who increased his profit on the job; the painters who didn't suffer health risks; and finally the environment since there was no toxic waste disposal, and no VOCs released into the atmosphere.

XIII. Operations

"We have a positive rule in every factory and branch that each crate and box must be opened carefully without breaking the wood....All scrap wood eventually gets back to the wood salvage department."
—Henry Ford, Businessman, 1926

Most of the extra thought that a sustainable building requires is expended during its design and construction. But for the building to achieve its full promise, it must be operated and maintained in accordance with its design.

Ideally, the building will have been designed to be easy to operate and maintain. Building operators should be intimately familiar with the environmental goals the building is meant to achieve. Occupants, too, should have a basic understanding of how their maintenance, purchasing, and daily activities will affect building performance. For example, selecting replacement lamps that do not have the same color rendition and performance characteristics as the original equipment may affect energy use, quality of light, thermal comfort, and productivity.

If the building is a house, the contractor or architect should thoroughly brief the owners about the building's systems, how they are intended to function, and how individual behavior affects the systems and building operations. Simple attitudinal and behavioral changes can be a critical factor in the success of an integrated system. For example, even the most efficient irrigation system can waste lots of water if it is run too often. Knowing how and when to operate a system correctly can prevent unnecessary waste, and it is not hard to learn—especially if the designers write operating instructions for both the maintenance staff and the occupants.

Maintenance

In most houses, there are a number of mechanical systems that require routine maintenance for optimal performance. In an office building, there may be a dozen or more. Each product's manufacturer provides specific instructions that explain what should be done to maintain the equipment and appliances found in any building.

Regular maintenance and inspection are essential to sustaining the efficiency of equipment and a healthy indoor environment. Heating, ventilation, and air conditioning (HVAC) system performance can be improved by insulating ducts and pipes, cleaning coils, filters, and registers, and maintaining programmable thermostats. Heat pumps, furnaces, and radiators will all perform better with regular cleaning and maintenance. Cleaning or changing the filters on a forced-air furnace once a month during the heating season will significantly improve its efficiency and indoor air quality. Be sure to flush all the water lines in a building after installation and before operating the system. Water heating performance can be improved by wrapping and insulating water heaters and pipes. And although efficient lights will require less frequent replacement, a regular cleaning schedule is still necessary, since the lamps are changed less frequently and may build up more dust.

If window air conditioners are used, it's important to clean and sterilize the condensate pan periodically. Fluid levels in solar hot water systems should be checked from time to time. Clean the condenser coils on refrigerators and air conditioners (dust and grime on the coils lowers their ability to shed heat). Check the bearings on ceiling fans; bad bearings or lack of lubrication can dramatically increase friction and energy use.

PURCHASING

Materials are bought to construct the building, and then the building occupants buy more materials and products to use and to keep a building running. The materials purchased can affect a building's energy and environmental performance. The first question to ask is: Is this product necessary? Is there another product that is already being used that could perform this task? How is this product packaged? Can the container be recycled, or can the product perhaps be bought in bulk?

Carefully study the building's operations and waste streams. Whenever possible, try to make sure that the items purchased are not making a "one-way trip" to the landfill. Specify recycled content for paper and other routine purchases. Purchase concentrated products and buy in bulk to reduce packaging. Choose chemical cleaning compounds with care; many conventionally formulated products have nasty effects on indoor air quality and in the waste stream. Alternatives to conventional products exist and do a good job. Magazines and catalogues featuring "non-toxic" products are available to help you make an informed choice.

RECYCLING

Americans produce an estimated 154 million tons of garbage—roughly 1,200 pounds per person—every year.[82] At least 50% of this trash could be, but currently isn't, recycled. Meanwhile, landfills in many areas are rapidly filling up and solid waste is a growing concern.

The volume of solid waste generated by a green building can be substantially reduced through source reduction, recycling, and composting. Investigate to see if recycling programs exist in your community. If they do, use them. If they don't, see if it's possible to implement them.

A space for recycling containers and a place for composting should be standard features in new homes. More than 80% of a home's waste comes from the kitchen, so consider placing the containers there or close by. Up to 30% of household waste is organic matter that can be composted and used to fertilize a garden, trees, or house plants. Commercial buildings can also easily incorporate provisions for convenient recycling.

Remember that occupants must pay for waste removal over the building's life. If, on the other hand, it's possible to reduce, reuse, and recycle, then the occupants of the building may also profit from lowered removal fees and the selling of recycled materials.

A Primer on Sustainable Building

XIV. Specification and Construction

"God is in the details."
—Mies van de Rohe, Architect, ~ 1930

If a green building is to perform as well as it can, the same commitment to sustainability must be maintained during the specification and construction phases as prevailed during the design. If anything, one must be even more vigilant.

During the specification period, it is common for substitutions to be proposed. Be certain that the substitutions are necessary and that the changes will not affect the energy and water efficiency, indoor air quality, or overall environmental performance of the building. Whoever is in charge of buying products or authorizing purchases must understand the importance of an integrated system. Remember that green design takes into account higher prices for some components in order to achieve much larger savings for the whole system. The innocent substitution of, say, lower-quality windows to "save a little" can end up costing a lot.

Energy efficiency can also be inadvertently subverted during construction. Careless work or inattention to detail—both common on jobsites—can wreak havoc with the best-laid plans. Installing fiberglass insulation is an unpleasant chore often delegated to the lowest-paid person on the job, but if the building is to perform up to specifications, it must be done with care. If the soffits are supposed to be caulked, somebody must see that they get caulked.

Be careful to protect the site's vegetation and other natural features during construction. Keep a close rein on heavy equipment operators. Don't clear more land than you absolutely have to. Flag trees to save. Designate parking, storage, and work areas, and provide a buffer between them and the landscape; a simple mesh fence may do. Also, provide a place for jobsite separation and recycling of construction debris.

Treat streams, creeks, and other watersheds with great care. The prevention of siltation, stream pollution, and topsoil loss is mandatory in many states and should be done regardless. Soil erosion prevention and control measures may be necessary, including straw-bale check dams, stone outlet structures, or silt fences.

Worker protection is another critical and oft-neglected issue. In the macho world of construction, workers are often treated as guinea pigs, exposed to all manner of toxic materials, paints, and finishes. Asbestos has been removed from most building products, but the jury is still out on whether long-term exposure to polyurethane varnish, to pick one example of many, is entirely benign. Most likely, it's not.

It is past time to pay more attention not only to the health of those who will live in the building, but those who *construct* it. Because a conscientious green designer will try to minimize the use of hazardous materials, a sustainable building jobsite should be a healthier place for carpenters, laborers, painters, and other tradesmen to work. Nonetheless, safety glasses, hearing protectors, dust masks, hard hats and other protective equipment will still be needed and should be used.

XV. CONCLUSION

*"...sustainable development is the Golden Rule for our children and
our grandchildren and their grandchildren."*
—PRESIDENT CLINTON, EARTH DAY ADDRESS, 1994

As you design and construct your green building, you are likely to find yourself educating others—contractors, subcontractors, tradespeople, and clients—who may not fully understand the concept of sustainable design. You may meet skeptical resistance to "ideas that no one has ever heard of." Stick to your guns. Some of the ideas presented in this book are new and somewhat controversial. It may help to remember that in the building profession, as in others, new knowledge often starts as heresy. Not too long ago, the average new house had single-pane windows and uninsulated walls. Whoever "pioneered" the use of double-paned windows and fiberglass insulation met with some skepticism, too. Now, these, in turn, are starting to be displaced by still newer materials. The fundamental principles underlying the green building movement are sound. Sustainable architecture is destined to grow. In time, it will be common practice.

As the builder or designer of a sustainable building, you have cost savings, energy efficiency, environmental preservation, and a host of other advantages to help convince skeptics. Green buildings will:

■ **Save energy:** Over 30% of the total energy and 60% of the electricity used in the United States is consumed in buildings. Modern energy efficiency can enhance any building's comfort, beauty, quietness, performance, bottom line, and worker productivity.

■ **Save water:** Water-efficient plumbing fixtures reduce water, energy, and sewage-treatment bills. They may also decrease tap fees while eliminating the need to dam rivers or expand water and wastewater treatment facilities.

■ **Promote economic development:** Resource-efficient buildings strengthen local, state, and national economies, since owners and tenants spend less money on imported energy and utilities. Those saved dollars stay in the community, supporting local jobs and businesses.

■ **Improve health and productivity:** Americans spend 80% of their time indoors. But it's hard to work smart in a dumb building or to stay healthy in a sick one. Owners of green office buildings report improved worker productivity and reduced absenteeism. Owners of green homes enjoy better air quality and health.

■ **Reduce pollution:** Saving a unit of electricity saves three or four units of fuel, generally coal, at the power plant. Burning less fuel reduces emissions of CO_2, the primary greenhouse gas, and SO_x and NO_x, which contribute to acid rain.

■ **Protect the environment:** Poorly designed or sited buildings scar the landscape, take valuable agricultural lands out of production, and blight wildlife habitat. Green buildings, on the other hand, can be designed to restore and enhance natural habitats. The use of recycled or sustainably sourced building materials can also help protect forests and endangered species.

■ **Enhance security:** Green buildings reduce dependence on precarious resource imports, improve trade balance and competitiveness, and create a fairer, more resource-abundant world.

■ **Benefit our descendants:** Green buildings make you feel better, not only because they're inherently more comfortable, but also because you're using up fewer of your grandchildren's resources and opportunities.

In conclusion, the measures introduced in this Primer can help create a beautiful, energy-efficient, aesthetically pleasing building or development that will use 50% to 80% less energy and water, produce correspondingly less pollution than a conventional one, possibly heal damaged environments, and promote healthy human and biological communities. In an age of increasing resource scarcity, those are eminently worthy goals. Green design is a good idea whose time has come.

Integrating the Principles in a Proposed Residential Project

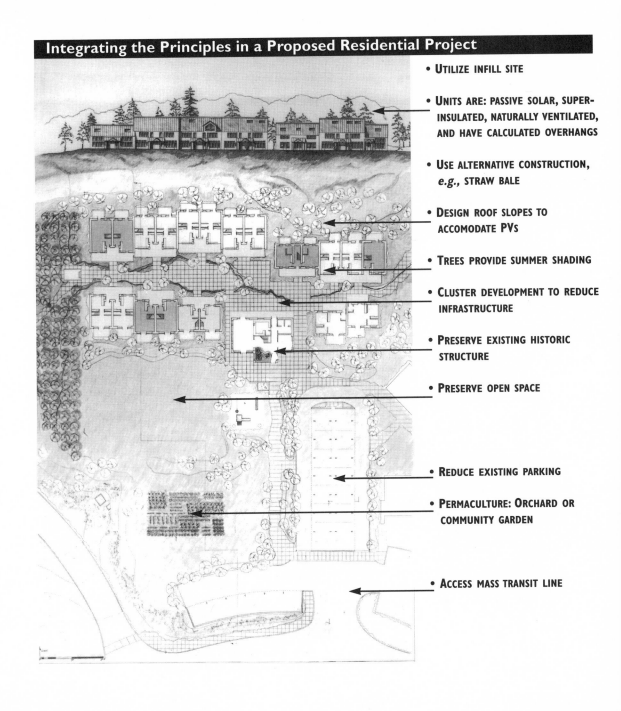

- **UTILIZE INFILL SITE**

- **UNITS ARE: PASSIVE SOLAR, SUPER-INSULATED, NATURALLY VENTILATED, AND HAVE CALCULATED OVERHANGS**

- **USE ALTERNATIVE CONSTRUCTION,** *e.g.,* **STRAW BALE**

- **DESIGN ROOF SLOPES TO ACCOMODATE PVs**

- **TREES PROVIDE SUMMER SHADING**

- **CLUSTER DEVELOPMENT TO REDUCE INFRASTRUCTURE**

- **PRESERVE EXISTING HISTORIC STRUCTURE**

- **PRESERVE OPEN SPACE**

- **REDUCE EXISTING PARKING**

- **PERMACULTURE: ORCHARD OR COMMUNITY GARDEN**

- **ACCESS MASS TRANSIT LINE**

A Primer on Sustainable Building

GLOSSARY

Active solar: A system using mechanical devices (pumps, fans, etc.) that transfers collected heat to the storage medium and/or the end-use.

Carrying capacities: The uppermost limit on the number of species and ecosystems or habitats possible given the supply and availability of nutrients in a given area.

Climate-dominated building: A building in which the energy consumption is driven by the heat loss or gain that moves across the building's envelope. The internally generated energy requirements from machines, appliances, or people are smaller than the energy requirements created by heat or cold moving through the building's envelope. This means that heating, cooling, and ventilation are the building's biggest energy requirement.

Cogeneration: The joint production and use of electricity and heat. Typically, electricity is the primary output of such large facilities as power plants. As a byproduct, heat can be used in food processing, district heating, or oil recovery. In contrast, industrial or small systems (e.g., laundromats, health clubs, and car washes) may be designed primarily to heat water while the generation of electricity is secondary.

End-use: The task or purpose for which energy is required. Examples include lighting dark spaces, cooking food, and powering vehicles.

Energy or water conservation: Using less energy or water. Conservation can imply a lifestyle change or a reduced level of service. Lowering thermostat settings or installing a shower flow restrictor are examples of energy conservation.

Energy or water efficiency: Using less energy or water to perform the same tasks. A device is energy-efficient if it provides comparable or better quality of service while using less energy than a conventional technology. Building weatherization or high-efficiency showerheads are efficiency technologies.

Green development: A sustainable approach to real estate development that incorporates such environmental issues as: efficient and appropriate use of land, energy, water, and other resources; protection of significant habitats, endangered species, archaeological treasures, and cultural resources; and integration of work, habitat, and agriculture. Green development supports human and natural communities and cultural development while remaining economically viable for owners and tenants.

Hydro (electric): Electricity that is produced when falling water turns generators. It is a renewable energy source derived from gravity and rain. Very small generation facilities, producing up to 50 kilowatts, are called micro-hydro.

Integrated design: A holistic process that considers the many disparate parts of a building project, and examines the interaction between design, construction, and operations, to optimize the energy and environmental performance of the project. The strength of this process is that all relevant issues are considered simultaneously in order to "solve for pattern" or solve many problems with one solution. The goal of integrated design is developments that have the potential to heal damaged environments and become net producers of energy, healthy food, clean water and air, and healthy human and biological communities.

Load-dominated building: A building whose energy use is driven by the internal loads like lighting, plug loads and heat from people. You can usually distinguish a climate-dominated building from a load-dominated building by whether or not the air conditioning is running year round, in a cool/cold climate. If the air conditioning runs throughout the year, it is probably load-dominated.

Passive solar: Systems that collect, move, and store heat using natural heat-transfer mechanisms such as conduction and air convection currents.

Pedestrian pocket (neo-traditional planning): Clustered housing, retail, and commercial spaces located within a quarter-mile walking radius of a transit system. This planning encourages walking, alternative transit, open spaces, and community, while providing affordable housing, local commerce, and reduced automobile traffic.

Photovoltaics (PVs): Solid-state cells (typically made from silicon) that directly convert sunlight into electricity.

R-value: A unit of thermal resistance used for comparing insulating values of different materials; the higher the R-value, the greater its insulating properties.

Renewable resources: Resources that are created or produced at least as fast as they are consumed, so that nothing is depleted. If properly managed, renewable energy resources (e.g., solar, hydro, wind power, biomass, and geothermal) should last as long as the sun shines, rivers flow, wind blows, and plants grow.

Retrofit: The replacement, upgrade, or improvement of a piece of equipment or structure in an existing building or facility.

Superinsulation: Insulating a building to minimize the amount of heat that can escape from (or, in a hot climate, enter) a building.

Superwindow: One of the new generation of glazing technologies, superwindows are double or triple-glazed window sandwiches which contain a center sheet of coated mylar "low-emissivity" film and are filled with argon or krypton gas. This construction and the coatings on the film allows short-wave radiation (visible light) to pass through, but reflects long-wavelength radiation (infrared or heat) so heat cannot pass through. R-values of 4.5 or more are achieved.

Sustainability: Meeting the needs of the present without compromising the ability of future generations to meet their own needs.

Weatherization: The process of reducing the leaks of heat from or into a building. It may involve caulking, weatherstripping, adding insulation, and other similar improvements to the building shell.

Wind power: Systems that convert air movement into mechanical or electrical energy. Driven by the wind, turbine blades turn a generator or power a mechanical pump.

Xeriscaping: Landscaping design for conserving water that uses drought-resistant or drought-tolerant plants.

APPENDIX A

LIST OF SOURCES FOR MORE INFORMATION

Energy Efficiency and Renewable Energy Clearinghouse (EREC)

Energy Efficiency and Renewable Energy Clearinghouse (EREC)
PO Box 3048
Merrifield, VA 22116
(800) 363-3732

Funded by U.S. Department of Energy, the EREC hotline provides a wide variety of information on renewable energy and efficiency measures. EREC has technical experts on staff that can answer questions on a wide range of energy efficiency-related subjects including practical implementation advice and sources of products and services. They also have an inventory of more than 500 publications, fact sheets, resource and referral listing, and bibliographies. Call or write them to receive a comprehensive listing of the services they offer.

Environmental Protection Agency (EPA)

Public Information Center
401 M Street SW
Washington, DC 20460
(202) 260-2080

The EPA provides an information service with referrals to various EPA hotlines and programs: radon, indoor air quality, asbestos, water quality, lighting, energy efficiency, EMF, and others.

Housing and Urban Development (HUD USER)

PO Box 6091
Rockville, MD 20850
(800) 245-2691

HUD USER maintains information on subjects that include public and assisted housing, building technology, community development, residential energy conservation urban infrastructure, environmental hazards, fair housing, and rehabilitation.

Lawrence Berkeley Laboratory (LBL)

Room 4000
1 Cyclotron Road, Bldg. 90
Berkeley, CA 94720
(510) 486-7489

LBL is a national research laboratory that does work on building energy analysis. Call for a list of publications and research papers.

U.S. EPA Green Lights Program

U.S. EPA
Green Lights 6202J
401 M Street SW
Washington, DC 20460
(202) 775-6650
fax: (202) 775-6680

The Green Lights program offers the most current information about energy-efficient lighting technologies and how to profitably upgrade your commercial building.

Weatherization Assistance Program (WAP)

US. Department of Energy
1000 Independence Avenue SW
Washington, DC 20585
(202) 586-2204

This office can put you in touch with your state economic opportunities office, which administers the Weatherization Assistance Program. The WAP helps finance home weatherization for low income families. Give your State Energy Office a try first though.

State Energy Offices may be your best source of free energy-efficiency information. Ask them to suggest an energy auditor or "house doctor." Most state energy offices will have detailed how-to booklets on insulation, weatherization, and furnace tune-ups as well as information on heat pumps, water heaters, solar applications, window insulation, etc. They can put you in touch with the state economic opportunities office, which administers the Weatherization Assistance Program. They also may be able to tell you where you can buy compact fluorescent lamps or efficient refrigerators locally. Give them a call. The toll-free numbers are in-state only.

	IN-STATE WATS NUMBER	DIRECT DIAL NUMBER
Alabama	(800) 452-5901	(205) 348-4523
Alaska	(800) 478-3744	(907) 563-6749
Arizona	(800) 352-5499	(602) 280-1402
Arkansas		(501) 682-1370
California	(800) 772-3300	(916) 654-5106
Colorado	(800) 632-6662	(303) 620-4292
Connecticut		(203) 566-5898
Delaware	(800) 282-8616	(302) 739-5644
District of Columbia		(202) 727-1800
Florida		(904) 488-6764
Georgia		(404) 656-5176
Hawaii		(808) 587-3800
Idaho	(800) 334-7283	(208) 327-7870
Illinois	(800) 252-8955	(217) 785-5222
Indiana	(800) 382-4631	(317) 232-8940
Iowa		(515) 281-4739
Kansas	(800) 752-4422	(913) 296-2686
Kentucky	(800) 282-0868	(502) 564-7192
Louisiana		(504) 342-1399
Maine		(207) 624-6800
Maryland	(800) 723-6374	(410) 974-3751
Massachusetts		(617) 727-4732

	IN-STATE WATS NUMBER	DIRECT DIAL NUMBER
Michigan		(517) 334-6261
Minnesota	(800) 657-3710	(612) 296-5175
Mississippi	(800) 222-8311	(601) 359-6600
Missouri	(800) 334-6946	(314) 751-7056
Montana		(406) 444-6697
Nebraska		(402) 471-2867
Nevada		(702) 687-4909
New Hampshire	(800) 852-3466	(603) 271-2611
New Jersey	(800) 492-4242	(201) 648-7265
New Mexico	(800) 451-2541	(505) 827-5900
New York	(800) 423-7283	(518) 473-4377
North Carolina	(800) 662-7131	(919) 733-2230
North Dakota		(701) 238-2094
Ohio	(800) 848-1300	(614) 466-6797
Oklahoma	(800) 879-6552	(405) 843-9770
Oregon	(800) 221-8035	(503) 378-4040
Pennsylvania	(800) 692-7312	(717) 783-9981
Rhode Island		(401) 277-6920
South Carolina	(800) 851-8899	(803) 737-8030
South Dakota	(800) 872-6190	(605) 773-5032
Tennessee	(800) 342-1340	(615) 741-2994
Texas		(512) 463-1931
Utah	(800) 662-3633	(801) 538-8690
Vermont	(800) 828-4069	(802) 828-2393
Virginia		(804) 692-3220
Washington	(800) 962-9731	(206) 296-5640
West Virginia		(304) 293-2636
Wisconsin		(608) 266-8234
Wyoming		(307) 777-7284

Alliance to Save Energy

1725 K Street NW, Suite 914
Washington, DC 20006-1401
(202) 857-0666

Provides materials on home energy rating systems, building codes, efficient new construction and design. Good videos on occupancy sensors, efficient lighting, etc.

American Council for an Energy-Efficient Economy (ACEEE)

2140 Shattuck Avenue, Suite 202
Berkeley, CA 94704
(510) 549-9914

ACEEE has joined forces with *Home Energy Magazine* to publish *The Consumer Guide to Home Energy Savings*, by Alex Wilson and John Morrill, now in its third edition (1993). This excellent resource is updated annually. It covers nearly all aspects of home energy use, including weatherization and insulation. Particularly useful are the listings of the most efficient new appliances. The book should be available at your local bookstore or by writing to the address listed above. Write ACEEE for a complete list of their publications on energy efficiency.

American Institute of Architects Committee on the Environment, Center for the Environment (AIA COTE)

AIA orders
PO Box 60
Williston VT 05495-0060
(800) 365-ARCH (2724)

The AIA is responding to the environmental challenge by promoting the role of architects, and other design professionals, in environmental decision making. Various projects and programs have been established to help guide architects towards sound ecological and economic decisions so as to create a sustainable society. AIA's Environmental Resource Guide is one of the best sources of information on green design and analysis of building materials. Call or write for more information.

American Solar Energy Society (ASES)

2400 Central Avenue, Suite G-1
Boulder, CO 80301
(303) 443-3130

ASES disseminates and transfers research on practical uses of solar energy, wind power and photovoltaics. Call them for a publications list.

Center for Resourceful Building Technology (CRBT)

PO Box 3866
Missoula, MT 59806
(406) 549-7678

CRBT's primary purpose is to perform research and educate the public on a variety of issues related to housing and the environment, with a particular emphasis on innovative building materials and technologies which place less stress on regional and global resources.

Center for Maximum Potential Building Systems

8604 FM 969
Austin, TX 78724
(512) 928-4786

"Max's Pot" has long been a leader in alternative building systems and materials research. Hands-on experience includes ecological land planning, building systems development, information systems management, and using regional resources to create appropriate materials. The center was instrumental in the creation of the City of Austin's Green Builder Program.

Energy Efficient Building Association (EEBA)

Northcentral Technical College
1000 Campus
Wausau, WI 54401-1899
(715) 675-6331

EEBA members are experts on building thermal performance, superinsulation and indoor air quality.

Energy Rated Homes of America (ERHA)

100 Main Street, Suite 404
Little Rock, AR 72201
(501) 374-7827

ERHA provides a high-quality home energy rating system coupled with and energy-efficient mortgage program.

Florida Solar Energy Center (FSEC)

Public Information Office, 300 State Road 401
Cape Canaveral, FL 32920-4099
(407) 783-0300

The FSEC offers a wealth of information on helping homes work in concert with the sun for heating, cooling, hot water, and electricity. Technical solar publications and house plans using renewables and efficiency are available.

Green Seal

1250 23rd Street NW, Suite 275
Washington, DC 20037-1101
(202) 331-7337

Provides free consumer information on the environmental impact of various types of appliances.

National Association of Energy-Efficient Mortgage Service Companies

3121 David Avenue
Palo Alto, CA 94303
(415) 858-0890

This association runs the Energy-Efficient Mortgage Program, which works to make it easier for home-owners to finance energy-efficiency improvements to their home.

Passive Solar Industries Council

1511 K. Street Suite 600,
Washington, DC 20005
(202) 628-7400

PSIC provides information on solar building design and retrofit issues, daylighting, insulation, and windows. Also available are excellent publications, software, and videos on passive solar design.

Rocky Mountain Institute (RMI)

1739 Snowmass Creek Road
Snowmass, CO 81654-9199
(970) 927-3851

Rocky Mountain Institute conducts research and outreach programs to foster the efficient and sustainable use of resources. RMI has seven program areas: Energy, Water, Agriculture, Transportation, Green Development, Security and Economic Renewal. Call for an information pack and a list of RMI's extensive publications.

U.S. Green Building Council

1615 L Street NW, Suite 1200
Washington, DC 20036-5601
(202) 466-6300

The U.S. Green Building Council, Inc. is a non-profit trade association whose primary purpose is to promote "Green Building" policies, programs, and technologies. Membership is offered to manufacturers, utilities, building owners, real estate advisors, scientific and technical organizations, and non-profit trade associations that are supportive of green buildings.

Magazines and Books

There are hundreds of books, trade journals, and research reports that deal with issues discussed in this Primer. Several publications that are consumer-oriented or useful to architects and builders interested in resource-efficient design are listed.

Magazines

Most of these specialty magazines are not available in local bookstores or libraries, so you may need to call or write the publishers.

Environmental Building News

RR1, Box 161
Brattleboro, VT 05301
(802) 257-7300

This is one of the best periodicals on sustainable building issues available. It examines environmental topics and the related aspects of building and materials. If you only buy one journal, make it this one.

Fine Homebuilding

Taunton Press
PO Box 5506
Newtown, CT 06470-5506
(800) 283-7252

This magazine publishes articles on innovative home designs and construction techniques.

Interior Concerns Newsletter

PO Box 2386
Mill Valley, CA 94942
(415) 389-8049

Information on environmental and materials issues for designers, architects, and building professionals are the contents of this newsletter.

Home Power

PO Box 520
Ashland, OR 97520
(916) 475-3179

A magazine about independent energy systems, photovoltaics, and renewable electricity options.

Microwave News

PO Box 1799
Grand Central Station
New York, NY 10163

The issues of electromagnetic fields and electricity are the focus of this periodical.

Books

Many of the following publications are available at local libraries and bookstores.

Prices are given for your information, however they may have changed after publication.

Alternative Energy Sourcebook

Real Goods Trading Corporation
966 Mazzoni Street
Ukiah, CA 95482
(800) 762-7323

A how-to and where-to-get-it guide all in one. This "comprehensive collection of the finest energy-sensible technologies" is 400 pages of information and items. ($14.00)

Builders' Field Guide to Energy Efficient Construction

Southern Electric International
Super Good Cents
64 Perimeter Center East
Atlanta, GA 30346
(404) 668-3445
Fax (404)668-3483

This book is an excellent source of tips and information on superior construction techniques, although it is focused on northwest building codes and climate. It also contains an excellent chapter on air/moisture barriers and sealing techniques, as well as ventilation design. Along with numerous drawings it will be very useful for architects, builders, and homeowners. (Free while supplies last.)

The Climate Change Action Plan

President William J. Clinton
Vice President Albert Gore, Jr.
October 1993

The President's plan to stabilize greenhouse-gas emissions contains over 50 initiatives, many of which affect the building industry and construction process.

Climatic Building Design: Energy-Efficient Building Principles and Practice

Donald Watson & Kenneth Labs
McGraw-Hill Book Company
Retail Services
Blue Ridge Summit, PA 17294
(800) 262- 4729

This book on solar gain, infiltration and ventilation, climate control, human comfort issues, and design strategies is interesting, technical, and amply illustrated . ($32.95)

The Community Energy Workbook

Rocky Mountain Institute
Alice Hubbard and Clay Fong
1739 Snowmass Creek Road
Snowmass, CO 81654-9199
(970) 927-3851

This workbook is a one-stop source for community activists and municipal development authorities to improve both the local economy and the environment by using a workshop process. It also addresses energy efficiency and tapping renewable sources, and includes worksheets. ($16.95)

Construction Materials Recycling Guidebook

Pamela Winthrop Lauer
Metropolitan Council, Attn:
Data Center
Mears Park Center
230 E Fifth Street
St Paul, MN 55101
(612) 291-8140

Practical suggestions for jobsite recycling is the focus of this book. Included is a bid specification guide that is adaptable for use anywhere in the country. (Free)

Consumer Guide to Home Energy Savings

Alex Wilson and John Morrill
American Council for an Energy Efficient Economy,
Publications Dept.
2140 Shattuck Avenue, #202
Berkeley, CA 94704
(510) 549-9914

The numbers book on energy efficiency. A must for anyone who wants to know just how much can be saved by using energy-efficient products, what they are, who manufactures them, and how to install them. It also lists performance ratings for most types of appliances. ($8.95 postpaid)

Creating Successful Communities
A Guidebook to Growth Management Strategies

Michael A. Mantaell, Stephen F. Harper, Luther Propst
The Conservation Foundation
Island Press
PO Box 7
Covelo, CA 95428-9901

A guidebook describing aspects of community development that includes consideration of environmental issues and provides strategies to protect the environment and successful communities. ($24.95)

Designing and Maintaining Your Edible Landscape Naturally

Robert Kourik
The Edible Landscape Book Project
PO Box 1841
Santa Rosa, CA 95402

A good book to teach you how to integrate food plants into a suburban yard. ($18.95)

The Earthbuilder's Encyclopedia

Joseph M. Tibbets
Southwest Solar Adobe School
PO Box 153
Bosque, NM 87006
(505) 252-1382

A thorough and practical book describing adobe and rammed earth construction. It provides details for foundations, roof construction, and even radon elimination systems. ($20.35)

EcoTeam Workbook

Global Action Plan for Earth
84 Yerry Hill Road
Woodstock, NY 12498
(914) 679-4830

A step-by-step program for groups or individuals who want to have a positive impact on the environment, starting with their own households. The book and start-up support are available with membership. ($38.00)

Efficient House Sourcebook

Robert Sardinsky
Rocky Mountain Institute
1739 Snowmass Creek Road
Snowmass, CO 81654-9199
(970) 927-3851

An annotated bibliography for anyone building, designing, or retrofitting a house. Lists state, Federal, and organizational sources of information, and reviews dozens of books and trade magazines on energy-saving home design and construction. 3rd Edition. ($13.95)

Energy Design for Architects

Alexander Shaw, Editor
The American Architectural Foundation
Fairmont Press
700 Indian Trail
Lilburn, GA 30247

A design resource for energy efficiency in buildings, written for architects. (Call for price)

Homemade Money

Richard Heede
Rocky Mountain Institute
1739 Snowmass Creek Road
Snowmass, CO 81654-9199
(970) 927-3851

A detailed description of what to do to retrofit an existing home, how to make it energy efficient, and how to prioritize among hundreds of cost-effective measures. Full of practical information and an extended bibliography with sources for more information. ($14.95)

Energy Efficient Windows

Ted Haskell
Oregon State University Extension Service
Administrative Services A422
Corvallis, OR 97331-2119
(503) 737-3311

Selection and installation of efficient windows are described in this publication, plus window energy efficiency ratings. ($1.50)

Energy: 101 Practical Tips for Home and Work

(also Recycling and Chemicals)
Susan Hassol and Beth Richman
Windstar Foundation
2317 Snowmass Creek Road
Snowmass, CO 81654
(970) 927-4777

These are well-documented books on what individuals can do to reduce energy waste at home, at work, and in transportation. ($4.00 per title)

Environmental by Design

Kim Leclair and David Rousseau
Hartley & Marks Inc.
79 Tyee Drive
Point Roberts, WA 98281

A relatively comprehensive guide to materials used for the interiors of buildings. Includes overviews of environmental issues. ($19.95)

Environmental Resource Guide

American Institute of Architects
PO Box 60
Williston, VT 05495-0060
(202) 365-ARCH(2724)

The ERG addresses environmental issues through reports on materials, case studies and special reports. Updated quarterly. Every design and construction office should have one. ($98.00 for AIA members, $ 165.00 for non-members)

Graywater Systems, Composting Toilets, and Rainwater Collection Systems: A Resource List

Rocky Mountain Institute
1739 Snowmass Creek Road
Snowmass, CO 81654-9199
(970) 927-3851

A resource guide for graywater, composting and rainwater collection technologies. ($7.00)

Green Architecture Design for an Energy-Conscious Future

Brenda and Robert Vale

Bulfinch Press

Little, Brown and Company

A thorough introduction to the issues of energy conscious building. Outlines environmental problems of conventional building and argues for resource-efficient design. For everyone who lives in, designs or builds a home. ($40.00)

Green Building Guide: A Sustainable Approach A Program of the City of Austin

Environmental and Conservation Services Department, 1992

PO Box 1088

Austin, TX 78767

A description of a pilot program in Austin Texas, this guide is an introduction to sustainability. It could serve as a model for other communities and for building rating systems. ($5.00)

Guide to Resource Efficient Building Elements, 4th Edition

Center for Resourceful Building Technologies

PO Box 3866

Missoula, MT 59806

(406) 549 7678

This is a great directory for recycled content and resource-efficient building materials. ($20.00)

The Hannover Principles: Design for Sustainability

William McDonough

William McDonough Architects

400 E Water Street

Charlottesville VA 22902

(804) 979-1111

Written for the World Exposition 2000, in Hannover, Germany, these guidelines will shape the development of the site. (approximately $10.00 for reproduction costs)

Healthy House Building: A Design and Construction Guide

John Bower

Healthy House Institute

7471 North Shiloh Road

Unionville, IN 47468

(812) 332-5073

A comprehensive book covering construction materials and building practices that may affect your health, plus a listing of less toxic alternatives. ($21.95)

Home Energy Briefs

Rocky Mountain Institute

1739 Snowmass Creek Road

Snowmass, CO 81654-9199

(970) 927-3851

A series of information packets on residential equipment and materials for consumers and homeowners. Titles to date include: Appliances, Refrigerators and Freezers, Water Heating, Windows, and Lighting. ($2 per title)

How to Build an Underground House

Malcolm Wells

673 Satucket Road

Brewster, MA 02631

A good introduction to building an earth-sheltered house. Contains planning ideas, practical instructions and clear illustrations. ($12.00 postpaid)

The Independent Home: Living Well with Power from the Sun, Wind and Water

Michael Potts

A Real Goods Independent Living Book

Chelsea Green Publishing Company

Post Mills, VT

An introduction to harvesting domestic power from the sun, wind, and water. Explanations of technologies and interviews are given by many people living "off the grid." ($17.95)

The Lighting Pattern Book for Homes

Lighting Research Center

Rensselaer Polytechnic Institute

Troy, NY 12180-3590

(518) 276-8716

This book discusses practical designs to help you see well and save money; details on energy-efficient lamps, luminaires, and controls; and plans for installing quality lighting in every room. ($50.00)

Living Community: A Permaculture Case Study at Sol y Sombra

Ben Haggard
Center for the Study of Community
4018 Old Santa Fe Trail
Santa Fe, NM 87505
(505) 982-2752

An inspiring description of the ecological restoration and permaculture project at Sol y Sombre in Santa Fe. (Call for price)

Making Space: Design For Compact Living

Rick Ball
Overlook Press
Lewis Hollow Rd
Woodstock, NY 12498
(914) 679-6838

Small houses are more resource-efficient than large ones—this book examines issues to help you make the most of small living spaces. ($18.90)

Manual For Building a Rammed Earth Wall

Lydia A. and David Miller
2319 21st Avenue
Greeley, CO 80631
(303) 352-4775

This manual details the Millers' experience with rammed-earth construction. Contains field-tested information, illustrations, and some designs. ($8.00)

The Massachusetts Audubon Society

Educational Resources Office
208 South Great Road
Lincoln, MA 01773
(617) 259-9500

Publications include: *All About Insulation; Building an Environmentally Friendly House; Contractor's Guide to Finding and Sealing Hidden Air Leaks; Financing Home Energy Improvements; Home Heating with Wood and Coal; Oil and Gas Heating Systems: Maintenance and Improvement; Saving Energy and Money with Home Appliances; Solar Ideas for Your Home or Apartment; Weatherize Your Home or Apartment.* ($3.75 each)

The Natural Habitat Garden

Ken Druse
Clarkson Potter/Publishers
New York NY

A beautifully illustrated exploration of gardens that are modeled on native ecosystems. Prairies, drylands, wetlands, and forests are all represented. ($40.00)

The Natural House Book

David Pearson
Simon & Schuster
Rockefeller Center
1230 Avenue of the Americas
New York, NY 10020
(201) 767-5937

A beautifully produced book on natural building and decorating materials, energy and resource issues, daylighting, and designing for feeling good in your home. ($19.95)

The New Solar Home Book

Bruce Anderson with Michael Riordan
Brick House Publishing Company
PO Box 134
Acton, MA 01720
(508) 635-9800

A comprehensive introduction to solar theory and technology. Includes appendices of climatic and design data. ($16.95)

The New Woodburners Handbook: A Guide to Safe Healthy and Efficient Woodburning

Storey Communications
PO Box 445
Pownal, VT 05261
(800) 827-8673

An informative book on stove selection, operation, proper wood, safety, maintenance, and installation. ($12.95)

Passive Solar Design Guidelines

Passive Solar Industries Council
Suite 1200
1090 Vermont Avenue NW
Washington, DC 20005
(202) 371-0357

A guidebook that details the basics of passive solar, sun tempering, direct gain, thermal storage mass walls, sunspaces, and natural cooling strategies. Contains site-specific information for 220 locations in the US. ($50.00)

The Passive Solar Energy Book

Edward Mazria
Rodale Press
Emmaus, PA 18098-0099
(215) 967-5171

One of the best passive solar books around, but it is now out of print. Try the library.

A Pattern Language

Christopher Alexander, et. al.
Oxford University Press

The second of a series of books that provide an alternative attitude to architecture and planning.($50.00)

Pedestrian Pocket Book: A New Suburban Design Strategy

Doug Kelbaugh, Editor
Princeton Architectural Press
in association with The University of Washington, 1989
37 E 7th Street
New York, NY 10003

An overview of pedestrian-based design that includes four proposals and illustrations. ($9.95)

Permaculture (A Designer's Manual)

Bill Mollison
AgAccess
PO Box 2008
Davis, CA 95617
(916) 756-7177

A classic text on how to grow food wherever you live. Used as a training manual, the text goes beyond permaculture design to address many environmental issues with good technical information and beautiful illustrations. ($39.95)

Plastered Straw Bale Construction: Super Efficient and Economical Buildings

David Bainbridge, Athena and Bill Steen
The Canelo Project
HCR Box 324
Canelo, AZ 85611

This introduction to straw-bale construction contains history and examples of this building method and details on how straw-bale buildings are put together. ($10.00 postpaid)

Rainwater Collection Systems

Morris Media Associate
4306 Wildridge Circle
Austin, TX 78759

A video and booklet combination that describing rainwater collection, systems, costs, and applications. ($29.95)

Reader's Digest Home Improvement Manual

The Reader's Digest Association
Reader's Digest Road
Pleasantville, NY 10570
(914) 241-5786

A manual that shows experienced do-it-yourselfers: how to draw plans, buy materials, estimate costs, get approvals, and complete every detail of the job. Also explains what's involved when hiring a contractor. ($28.00)

Residential Building Design & Construction Workbook

Ned Nisson
Cutter Information Corp.
37 Broadway
Arlington, MA 02174-5539
(800) 888-8939

A how-to workbook for building comfortable, energy-efficient homes, that discusses superinsulation, energy dynamics, and moisture control. Also discussed are the interrelationships between roofs, ceilings, walls, windows, foundations, heating, cooling, ventilation, and indoor air quality. ($95.00)

Shelter

Shelter Publications, Inc.
Home Book Service
PO Box 650
Bolinas, CA 94924

A unique source of information about simple vernacular styles for homes, natural materials, and resource use. ($16.95)

Solar Building Architecture

Bruce Anderson, Editor
MIT Press, 1990
Cambridge, MA

This book presents design fundamentals for energy efficient architecture. (Call for price)

The Sourcebook for Sustainable Design

Andrew St. John, Editor
Boston Society of Architects
52 Broad Street
Boston, MA 02109
(617) 951-1433 x 221

A comprehensive listing of products and materials to be used in sustainable building construction. Includes material listings and a resource guide of other information sources. ($19.95)

A Straw Bale Primer

S.O. MacDonald and Orien MacDonald
November 1991
PO Box 58
Gila, NM 88038

A good how-to booklet describing straw-bale construction methods. Includes information on Nebraska style and post-and-beam structures, a 10-step plan, and good illustrations. ($10.00)

Superinsulated Design and Construction: A Guide to Building Energy-Efficient Homes

T. Lenchek, C. Mattock, & J. Raabe
Van Nostrand Reinhold
115 Fifth Avenue
New York, NY 10023
(800) 842-3636

A good in-depth look at efficient building shell designs. Originally written in 1987, updated in 1992.

Tiny Houses: or How to Get Away From It All

Lester Walker
Overlook Press
Lewis Hollow Road
Woodstock, NY 12498
(914) 679-6838

Although "tiny" houses (the largest is 365 ft^2) may not be practical for everyone, this book focuses on economies of space with charming illustrations and descriptions of buildings. ($27.95)

Water Efficiency for Your Home

Rocky Mountain Institute
1739 Snowmass Creek Road
Snowmass, CO 81654-9199
(970) 927-3851

An informative brochure featuring products and advice that save water, energy, and money. ($1.00)

The Wood Users Guide

Rainforest Action Network
450 Sansome Suite 700
San Francisco, CA 94111
(415) 398-4404

A guide on alternatives to tropical hardwoods. Contains practical information of finding alternatives and a source listing. ($7.50)

The Xeriscape Flower Gardener
A Water Wise Guide for the Rocky Mountain Region

Jim Knopf
Johnson Publishing
1880 South 57th Court
Boulder, CO 80301

Although it is a regional book, many of the ideas are suitable for other climatic regions. ($14.95)

Your Home Cooling Energy Guide

John T. Krigger
Saturn Resource Management
324 Fuller Avenue, Suite S-8
Helena, MT 59601
(800) 735-0577

An informative guide about reducing cooling costs and improving comfort during hot weather. ($12.50)

Your Natural Home: The Complete Sourcebook and Design Manual for Creating a Healthy, Beautiful and Environmentally Sensitive House

Janet Marinelli and Paul Bierman-Lytle
Little Brown & Company
1271 Avenue of the Americas
New York, NY 10020
(212) 522-8700

This book provides real examples of environmentally responsible homes and apartments that are truly beautiful and healthy. Design options and green measures are presented for a variety of budgets. The book also reviews over 2,000 products for new construction, remodeling, and interiors, telling why they're important and how to get them. ($21.95)

A mail-order company may be your best, and sometimes only, source for some energy efficient technologies described in this book.

Eco-Source

9051 Mill Station Road, Bldg. #E
Sebastopol, CA 95472
(707)-829-7957

Offers environmental and biodegradable products in areas such as paper, recycling systems, and lighting. Also a good source for improving air or water quality, including air purification units and non-toxic materials.

Environmental Store

125 Pompton Plains Crossroad
Wayne, NJ 07470
(201) 616-0220

"Clean & Green" household products for all types of washing and personal care are available through this company. Everything is ecologically friendly in both testing and packaging.

Environmental Construction Outfitters Product Guidebook

Environmental Construction Outfitters
44 Crosby Street
New York, NY 10012
(212) 334-9659
(800) 238-5008

Offers an eighty-category listing of products and technologies researched and recommended by Environmental Construction Outfitters. Each category also explains the environmental issues associated with conventional products.

Green Pages

Andrew Fuston, Kim Plaskon Nadel
45 East 25th Street, 14th Floor
New York, NY 10010-2941

A listing of over 200 environmentally responsible or resource- or energy-efficient materials and products and their manufacturers, as well as contact information. This source book is updated semi-annually.

The Natural Choice Eco Design Company

1365 Rufina Circle
Santa Fe NM 87502
(505) 438-3448

A catalogue of environmentally friendly bedding, clothing, and housewares. A particularly good source for paints and finishes.

Real Goods Trading Company

966 Mazzoni Street
Ukiah, CA 95482
(800) 762-7325

Publishes the *Alternative Energy Sourcebook* which is full of information on photovoltaic cells, twelve-volt light fixtures, inverters, and various other devices for those wishing to escape from the utility grid. They also offer a diverse line of efficient household and yard items.

Resource Conservation Technology

2633 N Calvert Street
Baltimore, MD 21218
(410) 366-1146

Manufactures and distributes state-of-the-art building materials for contractors and technical professionals, for new construction and large remodeling jobs.

Seventh Generation

49 Hercules Drive
Colchester, VT 05446
(800) 456-1177

This free catalog contains many items for energy and water savings, including water-efficient showerheads, programmable thermostats, caulking, and test kits to detect radon.

APPENDIX B

Environmental Building News, Sept-Oct 1992

Checklist for Environmentally Sustainable Design and Construction

DESIGN

Smaller is better.	Optimize use of interior space through careful design so that the overall building size—and resource use in constructing and operating it—are kept to a minimum.
Design an energy-efficient building	Use high levels of insulation, high-performance windows, and tight construction. In southern climates, choose glazings with low solar heat gain.
Design buildings to use renewable energy.	Passive solar heating, daylighting, and natural cooling can be incorporated cost-effectively into most buildings. Also consider solar water heating and photovoltaics—or design buildings for future panel installation. If wood heating is an option, specify a low-emission wood stove or pellet stove.
Optimize material use.	Minimize waste by designing for standard sizes. Avoid waste from structural over-design (use optimum-value engineering/advanced framing).
Design water-efficient, low-maintenance landscaping.	Conventional lawns have a high impact because of water use, pesticide use, and pollution generated from mowing. Landscape with drought-resistant native plants and perennial groundcovers.
Make it easy for occupants to recycle waste.	Make provisions for storage and processing of recyclables: recycling bins near the kitchen, undersink door-mounted bucket with lid for compostable food waste, *etc.*
Look into the feasibility of graywater and roof-top water catchment systems.	Water that has been used for bathing, dish washing, or clothes washing can be recycled for flushing toilets or irrigation. If current codes prevent graywater recycling, consider designing the plumbing for easy future adaptation. Rooftop water catchment for outdoor watering should be considered in many regions.
Design for future reuse.	Make the structure adaptable to other uses, and choose materials and components that can be reused or recycled.
Avoid potential health hazards: radon, EMF, pesticides.	Follow recommended practices to minimize radon entry into the building and provide for future mitigation if necessary. Plan electrical wiring and placement of electrical equipment to minimize electromagnetic field exposure. Design insect-resistant detailing that will require minimal use of pesticides.

SITING

Renovate older buildings.	Conscientiously renovating existing buildings is the most sustainable construction.
Evaluate site resources.	Early in the siting process carry out a careful site evaluation: solar access, soils, vegetation, important natural areas, *etc.*
Locate buildings to minimize environmental impact.	Cluster buildings or build attached units to preserve open space and wildlife habitats, avoid especially sensitive areas including wetlands, and keep roads and service lines short. Leave the most pristine areas untouched, and look for areas that have been previously damaged to build on.
Pay attention to solar orientation.	Reduce energy use by orienting buildings to make optimal use of passive solar heating, daylighting, and natural cooling.
Situate buildings to benefit from existing vegetation.	Trees on the east and west sides of a building can dramatically reduce cooling loads. Hedge rows and shrubbery can block cold winter winds or help channel cool summer breezes into the building.
Minimize transportation requirements.	Locate buildings to provide access to public transportation, bicycle paths, and walking access to basic services. Commuting can also be reduced by working at home. Consider home office needs with layout and wiring.

<table>
<tr><td rowspan="11" style="writing-mode: vertical-rl;">**M A T E R I A L S**</td></tr>
</table>

Avoid ozone-depleting chemicals in mechanical equipment and insulation.	CFCs have largely been phased out, but their primary replacements—HCFCs—also damage the ozone layer and should be avoided where possible. Reclaim CFCs when servicing or disposing of equipment (required by law) and, if possible, take CFC-based foam insulation to a recycler who can capture CFCs.
Use durable products and materials.	Because manufacturing is very energy-intensive, a product that lasts longer or requires less maintenance usually saves energy. Durable products also contribute less to our solid waste problems.
Choose building materials with low embodied energy.	One estimate of the relative energy intensity of various materials (by weight) is as follows: Lumber = 1 Brick = 2 Cement = 2 Glass = 3 Fiberglass = 7 Steel = 8 Plastic = 30 Aluminum = 80.—Source: *Building and Environment* Vol.27 No.1
Buy locally produced building materials.	Transportation is costly in both energy use and pollution generation. Look for locally produced materials (local softwoods or hardwoods, for example) to replace products imported to your area.
Use building products made from recycled materials.	Building products made from recycled materials reduce solid waste problems, cut energy consumption in manufacturing, and save on natural resource use. A few examples of materials with recycled content are cellulose insulation, Homosote®, Thermo-ply®, and recycled plastic lumber.
Use salvaged building materials when possible.	Reduce landfill pressure and save natural resources by using salvaged materials: lumber, millwork, certain plumbing fixtures, and hardware, for example. Make sure these materials are safe (test for lead paint and asbestos), and don't sacrifice energy efficiency or water efficiency by reusing old windows or toilets.
Minimize use of old-growth timber.	Avoid lumber products produced from old-growth timber when acceptable alternatives exist. You may not need clear narrow-grained cedar or redwood siding, for example, when using an opaque stain or paint—as long as proper detailing is used to avoid rot. Laminated wood timbers can be substituted for old-growth Douglas fir. Don't buy tropical hardwoods unless the seller can document that the wood comes from well-managed forests.
Avoid materials that will offgas pollutants.	Solvent-based finishes, adhesives, carpeting, particleboard, and many other building products release formaldehyde and volatile organic compounds (VOCs) into the air. These chemicals can affect workers' and occupants' health as well as contribute to smog and ground-level ozone pollution outside.
Minimize use of pressure-treated lumber.	Use detailing that will prevent soil contact and rot. Where possible, use alternatives such as recycled plastic lumber. Take measures to protect workers when cutting and handling pressure-treated wood, and never burn scraps.
Minimize packaging waste	Avoid excessive packaging, such as plastic-wrapped plumbing fixtures or fasteners that aren't available in bulk. Tell your supplier why you are avoiding over-packaged products. Keep in mind, however, that some products must be carefully packaged to prevent damage—and resulting waste.

EQUIPMENT	Install high-efficiency heating and cooling equipment.	Well-designed high-efficiency furnaces, boilers, and air conditioners (and distribution systems) not only save the building occupants money, but also produce less pollution during operation. Install equipment with minimal risk of combustion gas spillage, such as sealed-combustion appliances.
	Install high-efficiency lights and appliances.	Fluorescent lighting has improved dramatically in recent years and is now suitable for homes. High-efficiency appliances offer both economic and environmental advantages over their conventional counterparts.
	Install water-efficient equipment.	Water-conserving toilets, showerheads, and faucet aerators not only reduce water use, they also reduce demand on septic systems or sewage treatment plants. Reducing hot water use also saves energy.
	Install mechanical ventilation equipment.	Mechanical ventilation is usually required to ensure safe, healthy indoor air. Heat recovery ventilators are preferred in cold climates because of energy savings, but simpler, less expensive exhaust-only ventilation systems are also adequate.
JOB SITE	Protect trees and topsoil during sitework.	Protect trees from damage during construction by fencing off the "drip line" around them and avoiding major changes to surface grade.
	Avoid use of pesticides and other chemicals that may leach into the groundwater.	Look into less toxic termite treatments, and keep exposed frost walls free from obstructions to discourage insects. When backfilling a foundation or grading around a house, do not bury any construction debris.
	Minimize job-site waste.	Centralize cutting operations to reduce waste and simplify sorting. Set up clearly marked bins or trash cans for different types of usable waste (wood scraps for kindling, sawdust for compost, etc.). Find out where different materials can be taken for recycling, and educate your crew about recycling procedures.
	Make your business operations more environmentally responsible.	Make your office as energy efficient as possible, purchase energy-efficient vehicles, arrange carpools to job sites, and schedule site visits and errands to minimize unnecessary driving. In your office, purchase recycled office paper and supplies, recycle office paper, use coffee mugs instead of disposable cups. On the job, recycle beverage containers.

APPENDIX C

Declaration of Interdependence for a Sustainable Future
UIA/AIA World Congress of Architects, Chicago, 18-21 June 1993

In recognition that:

A sustainable society restores, preserves, and enhances nature and culture for the benefit of all life, present and future;

- a diverse and healthy environment is intrinsically valuable and essential to a healthy society;

- today's society is seriously degrading the environment and is not sustainable;

We are ecologically interdependent with the whole natural environment;

- we are socially, culturally, and economically interdependent with all of humanity;

- sustainability, in the context of this interdependence, requires partnership, equity, and balance among all parties;

Buildings and the built environment play a major role in the human impact on the natural environment and on the quality of life;

- sustainable design integrates consideration of resource and energy efficiency, healthy buildings and materials, ecologically and socially sensitive land-use, and an aesthetic sensitivity that inspires, affirms, and ennobles;

- sustainable design can significantly reduce adverse human impacts on the natural environment while simultaneously improving quality of life and economic well-being;

We commit ourselves as members of the world's architectural and building-design professions, individually and through our professional organizations, to:

- Place environmental and social sustainability at the core of our practices and professional responsibilities.

- Develop and continually improve practices, procedures, products, curricula, services, and standards that will enable the implementation of sustainable design.

- Educate our fellow professionals, the building industry, clients, students, and the general public about the critical importance and substantial opportunities of sustainable design.

- Establish policies, regulations and practices in government and business that ensure sustainable design becomes normal practice.

- Bring all existing and future elements of the built environment—in their design, production, use and eventual reuse—up to sustainable design standards.

Olufemi Majekodunmi, President
International Union of Architects

Susan A. Maxman, President
American Institute of Architects

APPENDIX D

NATIONAL PLUMBING STANDARDS EXCERPT FROM CONGRESSIONAL RECORD, VOL. 138, NO. 142 PART V, OCTOBER 5, 1992.

Many suppliers and contractors are still using inefficient plumbing hardware, basically because they still haven't used up their stocks. Make sure you specify equipment that meets the following federal standards for plumbing fixtures. These were established by the Energy Policy Act of 1992, as reported in the Congressional Record, Vol. 138, No. 142 part V, October 5, 1992. Copies of the entire act are available for $11.00 postpaid by calling (202)783-3238 or by writing to the Government Printing Office, Superintendent of Documents, PO Box 371954, Pittsburgh, PA 15250-7954.

(j) STANDARDS FOR SHOWERHEADS AND FAUCETS.

(1) The maximum water use allowed for any showerhead manufactured after January 1, 1994, is 2.5 gallons per minute when measured at a flowing water pressure of 80 pounds per square inch. Any such showerhead shall also meet the requirements of ASME/ANSI A112.18IM-1989, 7.4.3(a).

(2) The maximum water use allowed for any of the following faucets manufactured after January 1, 1994, when measured at a flowing water pressure of 80 pounds per square inch, is as follows:

Lavatory faucets	2.5 gallons per minute
Lavatory replacement aerators	2.5 gallons per minute
Kitchen faucets	2.5 gallons per minute
Kitchen replacement aerators	2.5 gallons per minute
Metering faucets	0.25 gallons per cycle

(k) STANDARDS FOR WATER CLOSETS AND URINALS.

(1) (A) Except as provided in subparagraph (B), the maximum water use allowed in gallons per flush for any of the following water closets manufactured after January 1, 1994, is the following:

Gravity tan-type toilets	1.6 gallons per flush
Flushometer tank toilets	1.6 gallons per flush
Electromechanical hydraulic toilets	1.6 gallons per flush
Blowout toilets*	3.5 gallons per flush

(B) The maximum water use allowed for any gravity tank-type white 2-piece toilet which bears an adhesive label conspicuous upon installation consisting of the words "Commercial Use Only" manufactured after January 1, 1994, and before January 1, 1997, is 3.5 gallons per flush.

(C) The maximum water use allowed for flushometer valve toilets, other than blowout toilets, manufactured after January 1, 1997, is 1.6 gallons per flush.

(2) The maximum water use allowed for any urinal manufactured after January 1, 1994, is 1.0 gallons per flush.

*"Blowout" toilets are high-volume flushometer toilets usually used in stadiums, airports, and other heavy use sites. Most consume 4 gallons per flush, have a 4-inch trapway, and are wall mounted with three bolts.

APPENDIX E

ABATED EMISSIONS FOR SINGLE-FAMILY HOMES

The following information is extracted from *Negawatts for Ahmanson Ranch*, by William Browning and Rocky Mountain Institute, 1992.

This study included calculations of annual energy cost savings and potential emission abatements. Seven building types—single-family detached homes, townhouses, apartments, office buildings, retail spaces, a school, and a hotel—were modeled. California Title 24 energy standards were used to determine the baseline energy consumption of the buildings. The buildings were then modeled using different packages of measures to achieve greater levels of energy efficiency. For the figures cited in the text, a single-family home was modeled with the following characteristics:

Single-family homes modeled at 2,500 square feet with 2 stories:

Base Case, California Title 24, 1992

- Building orientation, west (270 degrees)
- R-30 ceiling insulation
- R-13 wall insulation
- Concrete slab, uninsulated, 20% exposed
- Glazing equal to 20% of floor area
- Metal-framed, double-glazed, slider windows
- 78% SE (minimum efficiency) gas furnace
- 10 SEER (minimum efficiency) central air-conditioning
- Interior white drapes
- Exterior shading on south and west facades
- 76% RE, 3.64% SB, standard 50-gallon, gas water heater
- Conventional lighting
- R-4.2 duct insulation

Advanced Efficiency Design Case: improvements over Title 24

- Building orientation, south
- R-43 ceiling insulation, with radiant barriers
- R-26 wall insulation
- R-7 slab edge insulation
- Glazing equal to 16% of floor area
- R-8, Hurd InSol-8 windows
- 95% SE gas furnace
- 15 SEER central air-conditioning
- Insulated doors
- Passive solar water heating, with on-demand backup
- Sun Frost refrigerator/freezer
- All high-efficiency lighting
- R-4.2 duct insulation
- Shading overhangs
- Light roof and wall color

Annual energy consumption per square foot, kBtu/ft²/yr
Single family detached home (2500 ft²)

End-Use	Supply Type	Title 24, 1992	Advanced House
Space Heating	gas	4.49	0.45
Space Cooling	electric	8.01	2.11
Water Heating	gas	7.76	0.91
Refrigerator	electric	1.46	0.35
Lighting	electric	0.90	0.30
Total		22.62	4.12
% Savings			82%

Potential savings were calculated at $.14/kWh (residential), and $.48/therm of gas. Potential emissions abatement through saved electricity was calculated by using data on the mixture of Southern California Edison's electric generation sources, and information on the emissions characteristics of various energy sources. This amounted to 1.52 lbs of avoided CO_2 per negawatt, .002 lbs of NO_x and .005 lbs of SO_x. Potential avoided emissions through saved natural gas was calculated as 11 lbs of CO_2 per therm.

Potential annual abated pollution for advanced house

	Gas, therms	CO_2 lbs/Home	Elect., kWh	NO_x lbs/Home	SO_x lbs/Home	CO_2 lbs/Home
Advanced	272.25	2,994.75	1,858.09	3.72	9.29	2,824.30
Over 30 years		89,842.50		111.60	278.70	84,729.00

Efficiency Measures	Total Annual Gas, therms	Annual Savings Electric, kWh	Energy Costs	per Household
Title 24	—	—	$501.48	—
Enhanced C - 82%	272.25	1,858.09	$124.14	$377
Savings over a 30 year mortgage			$11,310.00	

■ *All Costs Computed in 1992 dollars*

The calculations for electric carbon-dioxide emissions reductions are based on multiplying pounds of carbon-dioxide emissions abated by saved kWhs multiplied by the dispatch characteristics of the Southern California Edison Company (SCE) grid. SCE's electricity is produced from the following sources: 20% gas (with some oil), 20% nuclear, 13% coal, 3% hydro, and 44% purchased from independent power producers and other utilities.[83] This produces the following formula:

abated CO_2 = saved kWh * ((0.2*lbs/kWh-gas) + (0.2*lbs/kWh-nuclear) + (0.13*lbs/kWh-coal) + (0.03*lbs/kWh-hydro) + (0.44*lbs/kWh-national weighted average))

The calculations for the amount of CO_2 abated by saving electricity produced from various sources includes the actual production efficiency for converting the energy source to electricity, upstream effects, such as construction and fuel processing, and downstream effects, such as transmission and grid losses. The abated CO_2 accounted to saved electricity from various sources is as follows:

Coal   2.86 lbs/kWh saved
Oil   2.14 lbs/kWh saved
Gas   1.47 lbs/kWh saved
Nuclear   .10 lbs/kWh saved
Hydro   .01 lbs/kWh saved
National Weighted Average 1.89 lbs/kWh saved.[84]

Combining abated carbon-dioxide emission figures with SCE's dispatch data produces the following:

abated CO_2 = saved kWh * ((0.2*1.47lbs/kWh) + (0.2*0.1lbs/kWh) + (0.13*2.86lbs/kWh) + (0.03*0.01lbs/kWh) + (0.44*1.89lbs/kWh))

= saved kWh (0.29 + 0.02 + 0.37 + 0.0003 + 0.83lbs/kWh)

= 1.52 lbs CO_2 abated per kWh

The amount of carbon dioxide abated by not burning a therm of natural gas is estimated to be 11.0 lbs.[85] This amount added to the abated carbon-dioxide from reduced electric consumption produces the total emission reductions.

Abatement of sulfur-dioxide and nitrous oxides is modeled only for electricity produced from coal-fired generation. Data were not available for emissions from the combustion of gas or other fuels. The abated SO_x or NO_x per saved kWh was multiplied against the percentage by Southern California Edison and from the percentage of coal generation contained in SCE's purchased power (estimated from the national weighted average for electricity production). This produced the following equations:

abated SO_x = saved kWh* ((0.13*lbs/kWh-coal) + (0.44*0.18*lbs/kWh-coal))

abated NO_x = saved kWh*((0.13*lbs/kWh-coal) + (0.44*0.18*lbs/kWh-coal))

with the average emissions of SO_x as 0.02lbs/kWh-coal and NO_x as 0.01lbs/kWh-coal.[86]

NOTES

1 William McDonough, Design, *Ecology, Ethics, and the Making of Things*, a transcribed sermon, Cathedral of St. John the Divine, NY, NY, 7 Feb., 1993, p. 15.

2 Lewis Mumford, *The Highway and the City*, New American Library, NY, 1963, p. 170.

3 HRH The Prince of Wales, *A Vision of Britain: A Personal View of Architecture*, Doubleday, NY, 1989, p. 77.

4 Kim Hamilton and William D. Browning, "Village Homes: A Model Solar Community Proves its Worth," *In Context*, No. 35, p. 35. In 1991 dollars. Discussions with the developer in August 1994 reveal a 30% premium for Village Homes.

5 William D. Browning, *Green Development: Determining the Cost of Environmentally Responsive Development*, Master's thesis, Real Estate Development, Massachusetts Institute of Technology, July 1991, p. 64.

6 Green Development Services is currently conducting research on more than 80 examples of green buildings and developments in this country and around the world.

7 Evidence from leasing buildings rated by the Britain's Building Research Establishment Environmental Assessment Method indicates that tenants are willing to pay more for a green building.

8 William Browning, *Negawatts for Ahmanson Ranch*, Consulting Report, Rocky Mountain Institute, 1992, p. 1. California Title 24 energy standards were used as the baseline for the energy consumption of a single-family home. Efficiency measures were then modeled to enhance the building's energy performance. Projected energy savings of between 10% and 82% were possible using different packages of proven, "off-the-shelf" efficiency technologies.

9 Please see Appendix E for an extract of the report *Negawatts for Ahmanson Ranch*, showing assumptions and calculations.

10 Gary Nabhan, *The Desert Smells Like Rain*, North Point Press, San Francisco, 1982. William Booth, "A Stillness in the Trees," *Washington Post National Weekly* edition, 31 July–6 August, 1989, p. 3B. There has been a decline in the songbird population in North America. Although scientists are still debating the cause, human interaction with the environment is almost certainly a factor. The

issue is to distinguish between good and bad interactions with the environment, and to emphasize the good.

11 Fannie Mae and Freddie Mac allow higher mortgage-to-income ratios for energy-efficient homes. This allows people to buy several thousand dollars more worth of home than they otherwise could. For more information on Home Energy Rating Systems and Energy Rated Homes of America, please refer to the list of sources in Appendix A.

12 President William J. Clinton and Vice President Albert Gore, Jr., *The Climate Change Action Plan*, October 1993, outlines a specific initiative to promote energy-efficient mortgages and make them more widely available across the country.

13 Please refer to RMI's Economic Renewal Program for more information (see Appendix A).

14 Renew America, Searching for Success: Environmental Success Index (Washington DC, Renew America, 1991), p. 1.

15 From research by William D. Browning and Joseph Romm on a productivity study of *Greening the Building and the Bottom Line*, available from RMI November, 1994.

16 Ibid.

17 National Audubon Society and Croxton Collaborative, Architects, *Audubon House*, John Wiley & Sons, NY, 1994.

18 From Southern California Edison Consumer Information sheets, referring to a study conducted by Lawrence Berkeley Laboratory. The color of a building material must be considered in conjunction with the absorptivity and emissivity of the material. For example, a white asphalt-shingle roof will absorb more heat than a white aluminum roof. Light colors are generally better than dark colors for reducing heat gain, but whiteness to the eye is not a reliable indicator of infrared absorptance.

19 National Park Service, *Sustainable Design: A Collaborative National Park Service Initiative*.

20 For more information on Superfund sites, contact the Environmental Protection Agency (please see Appendix A).

21 *Environment and Development Newsletter*, American Planning Association, 1992.

22 Andropogon Associates, 374 Shurs Lane, Philadelphia, PA 19128.

23 Dewees Island Real Estate, Inc. 46 41st Avenue, PO Box 361, Dewees Island, SC 29451-2662.

24 John, Mott-Smith, *Residential Street Widths*, Solar California Local Government Commission, State of California, Sacramento, 1982.

25 Browning, *Green Development: Determining the Cost of Environmentally Responsive Development*, op.cit.

26 For more about positive spaces and an introduction to building and landscape design, see *A Pattern Language* by Christopher Alexander, Oxford Press, NY, 1977.

27 Shading in combination with a light-colored roof result in significant reductions in cooling load. The heat gained from a dark roof in cold climates is not enough to offset the unwanted heat gain in the summer. Lawrence Berkeley Laboratory, Berkeley, CA 94720.

28 For more information, please refer to *Permaculture*, by Bill Mollison. Please see Appendix A for source information.

29 Browning, *Green Development: Determining the Cost of Environmentally Responsive Development*, op.cit.

30 Lester Walker, *Tiny Houses*, The Overlook Press, Woodstock, New York.

31 Gregory Franta, Environmentally Sustainable Architecture in a Health-Care Facility, *AIA Environmental Resource Guide* article, April 1992.

32 From a speech by Randolph Croxton at the E SOURCE Members' Forum, 6 October 1993.

33 For example, there are some questions about whether or not fiberglass insulation may have a detrimental effect on indoor air quality. If you are designing for a person with multiple chemical sensitivity (MCS) this may be an important factor. An integrated design will also consider the life-cycle cost of different types of insulation.

34 Radiant barriers have very little R-value and little conductive resistance. They increase the effective R-value because they reflect radiant heat.

35 For source information on the Passive Solar Industries Council, please refer to Appendix A.

36 These windows are a proven technology with good results and good warranties. When correctly installed there is little concern about their not performing to standards. The gases do not dissipate and system

failure is rare.

37   Marianee Kyriakos, "Professor Finds Home Affects Moods, Culture," *The Washington Post*, 20 April 1994.

38   National Association of Home Builders *BMC West Dimensions*, Spring, 1994, p.8.

39   J.R. Cole and D. Ronsseau, "Environmental Auditing and Building Construction: Energy and Air Pollution Indices for Building Materials," *Building and Environment*, Vol. 27, No. 1, 1992.

40   Cynthia Crossen, "Tactical Research, Muddied Diaper Debate" *The Wall Street Journal*, 17 May 1994, p. B1.

41   The advantages of fluorescents are still believed to outweigh their disadvantages.

42   *Fine Homebuilding* #74, May 1992.

43   For detailed information on retrofitting an existing building, please refer to *The Energy Efficient Home*, available through RMI. Please see Appendix A for source information.

44   Straw-bale buildings have been tested for fire ratings and are suitable for Type 5 construction. Additional testing is being conducted. For more information, please refer to Appendix A.

45   A source for information on some alternative methods is *The Efficient House Sourcebook*. Please see Appendix A for source information.

46   Efficiency measures may also mean that plenum heights can be reduced, and that mechanical rooms can be smaller, which may give the building more usable square footage in the same building envelope size.

47   The Davis House was designed for Pacific Gas and Electric Company's Advanced Customer Technology Test for Maximum Energy Efficiency (the ACT2 experiment). For more information, contact PG&E Research and Development. (Appendix A).

48   It seems obvious why it makes sense to reduce your energy load when you are paying high rates. However, if you are installing your own power system, you should still reduce your energy load as much as possible. This will allow you to buy a much smaller system that is cheaper to buy, ship, install, and maintain.

49   Demonstrated savings of 3–5% have been shown in large commercial projects and in single-family homes. This information is taken from

research by RMI's Green Development Services on green architecture case studies.

50   E SOURCE *Technology Atlas: Space Cooling and Air Handling 6.6*, 1992, p. 101. The seasonal energy efficiency ratio is the seasonal cooling output in BTU divided by the seasonal energy input in watt-hours for a U.S. climate. Air conditioners are rated by these numbers, with a higher number being more efficient.

51   Ibid. Routine maintenance will help an air conditioner to run more efficiently. Basic maintenance procedures should include: cleaning all indoor and outdoor coils once a year; cleaning the blower and replacing filters at least once a year; and measuring refrigerant charge. The last procedure may need to be done by a certified technician.

52   Rocky Mountain Institute, *Visitor's Guide*, 3rd edition, July 1991.

53   Office of Technology Assessment (1992); *Building Energy Efficiency*, U.S. Congress, OTA-E-518, pp. 18 and 38.

54   Bigelow Homes, 999 South Plum Grove Road, Palatine, IL 60067.

55   E SOURCE *Technology Atlas*, op. cit., p. 22.

56   David Collier, Oregon Department of Environmental Quality, Woodstove Heating Program, Portland, personal communication, August 1993. New EPA-approved stoves are 267 times more polluting, and older stoves are closer to 1,000 times more polluting, than gas. Based on particulate matter consisting of carbon, condensable hydro-carbons, condensed organic PM10 in lb/million BTU of heat: wood = 2.5, oil = 0.02, and natural gas = 0.003, based on a mix of 80% conventional and 20% EPA–rated wood stoves. EPA-certified wood stoves are rated at 0.8 lb/million BTU.

57   "Electricity costs about 2.3 cents per 1,000 BTUs of delivered heat, while natural gas costs about 0.8 cents per 1,000 BTUs." Office of Technology Assessment (1992), *Building Energy Efficiency*, US, Congress, OTA-E-518, p. 39.

58   *Home Energy* magazine reports savings in excess of 20% with two eight-hour, 10 F° setbacks. Electronic thermostats are available for $25 to $150 at hardware and heating supply stores.

59   Office of Technology Assessment (1992), *Building Energy Efficiency*, U.S. Congress, OTA-E-518, p. 79.

60   E SOURCE *Technology Atlas*, op. cit., p. 24.

61   The color temperature or "warmth" of a light is measured in degrees Kelvin; 3500 Kelvin is a "warm" or yellow light that approximates

the light of an incandescent lamp. Kelvin ratings are found on the lamp packages. The rate of energy consumption by a lamp is measured in watts. The number of watts used by a lamp is also found on the packages. CFLs often have comparisons to standard incandescent lamps.

62 A good source for more information is *The Lighting Pattern Book for Homes*, (Appendix A).

63 Luminaire optics should be designed for the specific lamp being used, and vented to keep the lamp cool for maximum efficiency.

64 The Real Goods catalogue has a wide selection of CFLs and manufacturers. Please see Appendix A for more source information.

65 E SOURCE, *The State of the Art: Water Heating, 4.4 Tankless Water Heaters*, 1990, p. 260.

66 E SOURCE, *The State of the Art: Water Heating, 4.1 Passive Solar Systems*, p. 225- 236, Appendix I: Basics of Solar Water Heating, p. 391, and Appendix E: Passive Solar Water Heater Manufacturers, p. 373, excerpts, 1990.

67 Check with your state's energy office to see if tax incentives are available.

68 E SOURCE, *The State of the Art: Water Heating, 4.1 Passive Solar Systems*, op cit., p. 250.

69 Energy efficiency and price are not correlated. Some energy "pigs" are more expensive than other similar appliances that use much less energy.

70 Four-fifths of a refrigerator's CFC content is in the foam insulation.

71 Rocky Mountain Institute, *Water-Efficient Technologies: A Catalog for the Residential/Light Commercial Sector*, Second Edition, 1993, p. 179. Alex Wilson, *Consumer Guide to Home Energy Savings*, American Council for an Energy-Efficient Economy, Washington, DC and Berkeley, California, 1991, p. 197.

72 ANSI has a rating system for copiers. Efficiency features to look for include an energy savings or standby mode that cuts in automatically after a set number of minutes and that turns the fuser heater to a much lower temperature.

73 Although not if it displaces a UPS for a critical application.

74 Real Goods, located in Ukiah, CA, is perhaps the largest retailer of residential PV systems in this country, and a good contact for

detailed information about sizing and installation of a PV system.

75 For more information on the different spray styles available, please refer to Rocky Mountain Institute's *Water-Efficient Technologies: A Catalog for the Residential/Light Commercial Sector*, 2nd edition, 1993.

76 Jim Knopf, 320 Hollyberry Lane, Boulder, CO 80303.

77 For further information on water-efficient technologies, please refer to *Water-Efficient Technologies*, op. cit.

78 Ecological Engineering Associates (EEA), and Ocean Arks International (OAI), a non-profit group which does the research for EEA, were founded by John Todd. They have had success treating both fresh and salt water.

79 Another exception might be for a home on a site that could not pass a "percolation test" for septic systems, and hence would be unbuildable without an alternative approach.

80 Multiple chemical sensitivity (MCS)/environmental illness (EI) is recognized as a disability by the Social Security Administration. MCS can be caused by some of the chemicals associated with construction, like formaldehyde. Since breathing is affected by MCS/EI, new regulations about indoor air quality may be issued in the near future. For sources of more information, please refer to Appendix B.

81 To obtain a copy of these standards, call ASHRAE at 404-636-8400.

82 This is enough garbage to fill the New Orlean's Superdome from top to bottom twice each day.

83 Paul Skvarna, Southern California Edison Company Research Center. These data are based on annual SCE generation statistics.

84 H. Richard Heede, *Carbon-dioxide Emissions Per Kilowatt-hour Consumed*, Draft Paper, Rocky Mountain Institute. These data are based on a series of calculations from information by the Environmental Protection Agency, Lawrence Berkeley Laboratories, Department of Energy/Energy Information Agency (EIA), and Richard Ottinger of Pace University Law School.

85 Union of Concerned Scientists estimate based on averaged carbon content for gas with capacity of 100,000 Btu.

86 Amory Lovins, "How a Compact Fluorescent Lamp Saves a Ton of CO_2," Rocky Mountain Institute, 1990. These numbers are derived form EPA National Air Pollutant Emission Estimates, and the Department of Energy's Annual Review of Energy, 1988.

TALK TO US!

We want to learn from you. Please give us your comments on this book and any thoughts you have on how to improve it by filling out this survey and mailing it to us.

Where did you hear about the book?

Did you find it useful?

Well organized?

What information is the book missing?

How many measures did you implement as a result of reading this book?

Which ones?

Did you find the book motivating?

Other comments:

ORDER FORM

Rocky Mountain Institute
1739 Snowmass Creek Road
Snowmass, CO 81654-9199
(970) 927-3851 / FAX (970) 927-3420
EMAIL: orders@rmi.org

Please send me the following RMI publications:

D95-2	*A Primer on Sustainable Building*	$16.95
E95-3	*Homemade Money: How to Save Energy and Dollars in Your Home*	_____ $14.95
E92-9	*The Efficient House Sourcebook*	_____ $13.95
ER95-4	*The Community Energy Workbook*	_____ $16.95
W95-36	"Water Efficiency for Your Home"	_____ $ 1.00

Home Energy Briefs *(circle titles ordered)*   _____

  E95-8 "Lighting" E95-10 "Refrigerators & Freezers"

  E95-9 "Windows" E95-11 "Water Heating"

  E95-12 "Cooking Appliances and Dishwashers"

  E95-13 "Washers, Dryers, & Misc. Appliances" $ 2.00 each or

  E95-14 "Computers & Peripherals"   _____ $10.00 for all seven

RMI *Newsletter* (three issues, one year)   _____ $10.00 *

RMI Publications Catalog   _____ Free

*requested minimum donation

subtotal: _____

shipping/handling (see chart): _____

+ 3% tax *if shipped to Colorado*

total enclosed: _____

Shipping & Handling Charges		
Order Amount	U.S.	Canada
$0.00–12.00	$2.50	$3.00
12.01–20.00	3.50	4.50
20.01–35.00	4.50	5.50
35.01–50.00	6.00	7.50
50.01–100.00	7.00	9.00

For charges on orders over $100, express delivery, or shipments outside the United States and Canada, please call, fax, or e-mail RMI's Publications Department. All charges are in U.S. currency.

☐ *My check or money order is enclosed*

☐ *Please charge my:* ☐ *Visa* ☐ *Mastercard*

*Signature:*_____

Card #: _____

*Exp. date:*_____

Please send the publications to: (please print or type)

Name: _____

*Address:*_____

Town/City: _____ *State:* _____

ZIP/Postal code: _____ *Country:* _____

Telephone: _____

135